Steffen Achenbach

Web 2.0. The New Showroom for Fashion Brands: How important is Social Media for the Fashion Industry?

GRIN Verlag

Bibliografische Information der Deutschen Nationalbibliothek:

Die Deutsche Bibliothek verzeichnet diese Publikation in der Deutschen National-
bibliografie; detaillierte bibliografische Daten sind im Internet über http://dnb.d-
nb.de/ abrufbar.

Dieses Werk sowie alle darin enthaltenen einzelnen Beiträge und Abbildungen
sind urheberrechtlich geschützt. Jede Verwertung, die nicht ausdrücklich vom
Urheberrechtsschutz zugelassen ist, bedarf der vorherigen Zustimmung des Verla-
ges. Das gilt insbesondere für Vervielfältigungen, Bearbeitungen, Übersetzungen,
Mikroverfilmungen, Auswertungen durch Datenbanken und für die Einspeicherung
und Verarbeitung in elektronische Systeme. Alle Rechte, auch die des auszugsweisen
Nachdrucks, der fotomechanischen Wiedergabe (einschließlich Mikrokopie) sowie
der Auswertung durch Datenbanken oder ähnliche Einrichtungen, vorbehalten.

Imprint:

Copyright © 2012 GRIN Verlag GmbH
Druck und Bindung: Books on Demand GmbH, Norderstedt Germany
ISBN: 978-3-656-66698-1

This book at GRIN:

http://www.grin.com/en/e-book/274720/web-2-0-the-new-showroom-for-fashion-
brands-how-important-is-social-media

GRIN - Your knowledge has value

Der GRIN Verlag publiziert seit 1998 wissenschaftliche Arbeiten von Studenten, Hochschullehrern und anderen Akademikern als eBook und gedrucktes Buch. Die Verlagswebsite www.grin.com ist die ideale Plattform zur Veröffentlichung von Hausarbeiten, Abschlussarbeiten, wissenschaftlichen Aufsätzen, Dissertationen und Fachbüchern.

Visit us on the internet:

http://www.grin.com/

http://www.facebook.com/grincom

http://www.twitter.com/grin_com

LONDON
SOUTH BANK
UNIVERSITY

WEB 2.0 - THE NEW SHOWROOM FOR

FASHION BRANDS: HOW IMPORTANT IS

SOCIAL MEDIA FOR THE FASHION INDUSTRY?

Steffen Achenbach

December 2012

A Dissertation submitted in partial fulfilment of the
requirement for M.Sc. International Business
London South Bank University
Faculty of Business

Declaration

I hereby declare that this dissertation is the result of my own independent investigation, except where I have indicated my indebtedness to other sources.

I hereby certify that this dissertation has not been accepted in substance for any other degree, nor is it being submitted currently for any other degree.

M.Sc. Dissertation Entitled:

The importance of social media for the Fashion Industry. An observation of 12 fashion brands and their activity on social media platforms.

Word Count: 20,500

Candidate Name, Surname: ....

Candidate Signature: ....

Date: ....

Acknowledgements

A special thank you to my supervisor Susan Avril Platt, Programme Manager Business Foundation and Access Courses at London South Bank University, for her valuable guidance and assistance during the entire dissertation process.

"The world as we have created it is a process of our thinking. It cannot be changed without changing our thinking."

-Albert Einstein-

Abstract

Internet technology has greatly changed in form over the past few years. What was once mainly used as a source of information is now an important communication tool in people's lives. Enterprises are increasingly using the internet and social media platforms like Facebook, Twitter and YouTube for their business communication to promote, to as many consumers as possible, their services and products. There are a variety of different ways enterprises can include social media in their business strategy. However, not every business is managing its social media presence effectively enough to maximise its benefits. Marketers often do not know how to deal with issues such as social media monitoring or creating brand awareness and shy away. In particular, the fashion industry shows a low level of social media engagement. Thus, the overall aim of this study is to investigate the importance of social media for the fashion industry. 12 international fashion brands were observed on a daily basis within one month to measure their social media activity. Furthermore, a user questionnaire and interviews with marketers were used to test the findings of the observations as well as from secondary literature. Thereby, the use and hence the engagement of brands with social media differ widely within the fashion industry. Some brands are aware of the impact social media can have on their business, whereas other brands prefer to use traditional (offline) marketing tools to engage with consumers. To survive on the future market, marketers need to change their thinking and integrate offline as well as online tools in their marketing strategy. The fashion industry has a high potential to use social media effectively to communicate new styles and trends. Due to its accessibility to photos and videos, social media enables fashion brands a fast and easy way of creating brand awareness and sharing advertising campaigns. Based on the findings, the researcher is able to formulate an overall strategic social media plan for businesses to improve their social media use and implementation. Additionally, the researcher developed within this study an innovative new social media measurement method which helps to determine a brand's performance on social media platforms.

Table of Contents

Index of Tables

Index of Figures

Abbreviations

e.g.	~	for example
cf.	~	compare
SMP	~	Social Media Performance

1 Introduction

1.1 Background of the Dissertation Topic

Over the course of the past few years, the Internet has greatly changed in form. From a pure source of information, the Internet has developed into a new mass-communication medium which offers numerous possibilities for the user to create, form and influence content. The Internet has become an important component of everyday life for many people. The steadily rising number of users and technological progress has pushed the Internet to develop from its static form into today's interactive Web 2.0. This allows communication and the exchange of opinions through social media platforms such as chat rooms, news forums or blogs (Fisch and Gscheidle, 2008). These new forms of communication in the so-called "social networks" have strongly influenced the formation of public opinion. While before only established media such as TV, newspapers or magazines could reach the public, a communication network was created by the establishment of Web 2.0 which offers the user the possibility to find an audience both nationwide and internationally. Consequently everyone is able to transmit positive and negative opinions, interests and events, both consciously and unconsciously to a huge number of people (Busemann and Gscheidle, 2009).

It has become easier, especially for enterprises, with this new form of the Internet as a data carrier and "key to every household" to market their products and services directly to the consumer. Here it must be noted that not only the intended opinion of the enterprise, but also the views of every user can be responsible for the formation of public opinion about a brand or product (Absatzwirtschaft, 2010b). It is necessary to clarify who the leading initiator of public opinion is, who can be affected by it and which factors have a decisive influence on opinion creation. This "word-of-mouth marketing", according to Misner (1999, p. 26) is the most current marketing measure and is able, in association with social media, to diversify and authoritatively influence the purchasing decisions of the affected persons.

Enterprises are increasingly using Web 2.0's new instruments in their business communication. They use the Internet with the help of content-orientated platforms such as Facebook, Twitter and YouTube, or the mechanisms which these platforms provide, to persuade as many consumers as possible about their offered services and products. Analysis and observation are also of great importance for enterprises, primarily to gain helpful information about their own products or the company from the broadly formed opinion of the masses (Absatzwirtschaft, 2010a). Particularly in the area of the social networks, a potential in the form of online advertisement exists for enterprises to pursue effective brand communication. On these platforms, the type of communication plays an important role as in Web 2.0 and especially on social networks an advertising banner is not enough anymore to successfully pursue brand communications. Marketers must focus more on the interaction with the user and pursue advertisement in a more dialogical form (Absatzwirtschaft, 2010b).

The past years have offered many examples of companies who communicated the wrong way with their users using social media because of ignorance and incomprehension of the main purpose of social media applications. One of the latest examples comes from the luxury fashion label Louis Vuitton. After a user created a parody to criticise the brand's image, the only thing Louis Vuitton did was to threaten the user and to sue him for defamation (Owyang, 2012d). There was no real dialog with the user. As more and more people joined in the conversation against the brand, Louis Vuitton learned the hard way that social media was made for people, not for brands (Fournier and Avery 2011, p. 193).

However, the traditional British clothing brand Burberry has gained a competitive advantage by using the opportunities offered by Web 2.0. When users enter the Burberry website, they begin a journey. Users around the world can view 3D live broadcasts of runway shows and at the click of a mouse, directly order the viewed item. Due to the innovative use of Web 2.0 and its social media platforms, Burberry has grown in new markets such as China in addition to their traditional markets (Business Today, 2011).

But it is questionable whether Burberry's successful integration of social media really led to their increase in market share and brand awareness. Furthermore whether their strategy to gain a competitive advantage can really be seen as a long-term strategy. Moreover whether this successful integration can be transferred to other fashion brands in a lower-priced sector.

Hence, the overall question is whether social media is the new "vogue" and important for the fashion industry. If yes, and if it is profitable, should companies increase their investment in it as Burberry did to gain competitive advantages and to enter new emerging markets? Does social media enhance brand perception and brand awareness? If not, why do companies then invest in it?

1.2 Demarcation of the Topic

To analyse the importance of social media for fashion brands, it is necessary to start by clarifying the terms "Web 2.0" and "social networks" in a more detailed way. A big impact on their importance is also today's most discussed question: Who really owns the influence? Do marketers still have power over their products due to the fact that social media has empowered the customers? Hence this includes a closer look at the diffusion process of innovations and who the leading initiator of public opinion is (as mentioned earlier), who can be affected by it and which factors have a decisive influence on opinion creation. With this qualitative background knowledge the importance of social media for fashion brands can be better researched, and hence conclusions can be made about whether companies should increase their investment in social media in the future.

1.3 Research Purpose

The main purpose of this study is to estimate the importance of the social media use for the fashion industry. This is driven by a previous study and published article by Socialbakers (2012c) about the response rate of different kinds of industries on Facebook. The concluded study indicates that the engagement of the fashion industry with social media applications is rather low and less responsive compared to other industries (cf. Socialbakers, 2012a). However, the potential for a successful and efficient implementation of social media applications in the business strategy of fashion companies is rather high. Users want to talk about fashion by using the

Web 2.0 and keeping up to date with the latest trends and products available on the market, as well as sharing their opinions online (Weber, 2012). Therefore this study was created to find explanations to what prevents fashion brands from improving their social media presence and from including it in their business strategy.

Additionally during the research process the purpose of this study changed in its form. The importance of social media was still the main objective to determine, but weaknesses in the measurement of companies' social media activity were also identified. Previous secondary literature has shown that companies struggle with analysing weather their social media activities are successful and efficient (cf. Marketingcharts, 2012). Hence it became important to develop an efficient strategy for businesses to overcome these weaknesses. Figure 1. illustrates the findings in a bar chart.

Figure 1. Measuring Social Media's Impact

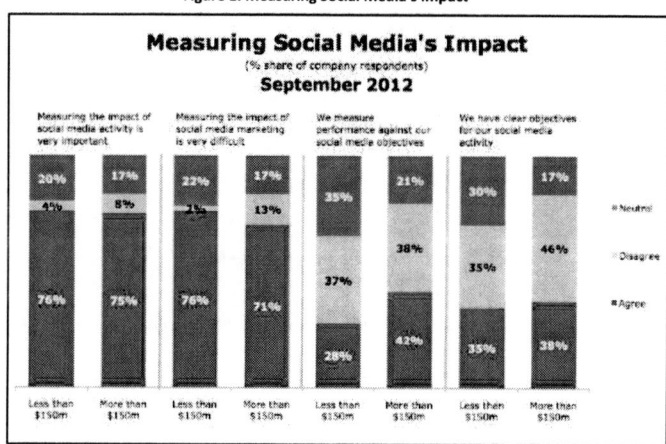

Source: Marketingcharts (2012)

1.4 Research Aim and Major Objectives

Due to Figure 1. in the previous section, the overall aim of this study is to address the following research question:

"How important is the use of social media for the fashion industry?"

4

The following nine objectives have been posited in order to address the research question:

(1) To clarify why the engagement of the fashion industry with social media is low.

(2) To find an efficient way to measure companies' social media performance.

(3) To evaluate if companies should increase their investment and include social media as a marketing strategy.

(4) To develop an effective social media performance strategic plan.

(5) To analyse if social media increases market share and brand awareness.

(6) To establish why one brand grows faster by getting more "Fans" than others.

(7) To evaluate the similarity between different brand's social media behaviour.

(8) To describe the differences or similarities in age and income of the users between the brands.

(9) To clarify who are opinion leaders and own the influence of opinion creation.

Supportingly to the main research question "How important is the use of social media for the fashion industry?" and to accomplish the research objectives efficiently, six research questions were defined to avoid errors during the research process and to keep the focus on the purpose of the study.

(1) How is success in terms of social media defined and how can it be measured?

(2) Is it profitable to invest in social media and should it be included in the company's long term marketing strategy to gain a competitive advantage?

(3) How can the use of social media be successfully implemented in the long term strategy of a company?

(4) What would a general guideline for a successful implementation into a company's business strategy look like?

(5) Does social media enhance brand perception and brand awareness?

(6) How do fashion brands use social media and what is their main purpose of using it?

These questions as well as the aims and objectives of this study will be analysed and evaluated in the discussion section of chapter 5 after outlining the results of the research process.

1.5 Structure of the Dissertation

This dissertation consists of six parts, including the introductory chapter. The following chapter provides a critical review of the existing literature in the field of social media and begins by giving basic definitions relevant to the topic. Furthermore the chapter looks at who owns the influence in opinion creation on social media platforms and the power struggles between marketers and users. Finally the third section discusses different methods to measure social media activity.

Chapter three describes the methodological approach; covering issues such as research design, data collection, sample selection and data analysis methods. Possible limitations concerning the research approach are also mentioned.

In chapter four, the twelve observed fashion brands are described and categorised in three different price genres. The chapter begins with a short definition of the term "Brand" and explains this in context to brand awareness and brand engagement. Subsequently, the study's findings will be outlined and discussed in chapter five. Within the discussion section, a new social media measurement method will be presented together with a strategic guideline for the successful implementation of social media into a company's business activities. The sixth and final chapter comprises the conclusions regarding the study's purpose and recommendations for future studies.

2 Literature Review

2.1 Introduction

The literature herein serves as a basis for the research questions that will be considered in this study. This chapter refers to the previous academic work about Web 2.0 and social media. The chapter is divided in three sections. Section one provides a review of the theoretical background of Web 2.0 and social media. This part analyses the different aspects of this new form of Internet based on a paper by Tim O'Reilly (2005), who stamped the term "Web 2.0" in 2004 for the first time. The importance lies in understanding what the term "Web 2.0" defines, how it changed the way of communication and how it is structured. This is necessary to analyse the importance and use of social media in the fashion industry, because the focus for the research is on special social media applications. Section two refers to the question of who owns the influence in the communication process and discusses (with detailed examples from previous works) the main issues brands are challenged with in using social media. This leads to a discussion about whether companies should increase their investment in the new technology. The last section of this chapter discusses the importance of the measurement of social media engagement as well as the methods used by different authors. An exact definition of the term "Brand" will be given in chapter 4, together with an explanation of brand awareness and brand engagement.

2.2 Web 2.0 and Social Media

Web 2.0 forms the basis for the diffusion of information through social media platforms. The technology of Web 2.0 permitted the rise of social media applications such as YouTube, Facebook or Twitter. Due to the development of this new form of the Internet, new ways of communication were created, which influence (besides the traditional media) today's opinion formation (Stanoevska-Slabeva, 2008).

7

Tim O'Reilly (2005) coined the term "Web 2.0" for the first time in 2004 at the "Web 2.0 Conference", and he has been, since that time, the name giver for this new development of the Internet (O'Reilly, 2005). O'Reilly and Dale Dougherty, the vice president of the O'Reilly publishing company, recognised during a brainstorming session that the Internet had not broken down during the bursting of the dotcom bubble in 2000, but had become more and more meaningful. After the conference, during which the central subjects were Web 2.0 and the changes linked with it on the Internet, O'Reilly published the article "What is Web 2.0?" the following year. With this article, he defines, above all, the concept of the new Web and characterises it in a more detailed way. He describes different aspects which decisively declares the Internet to be in this new form and especially explains the basis for the diffusion of information in the net (O'Reilly, 2005).

The central aspects of his report form, in particular, the representation of the Web as a platform, and the inclusion linked with it, of the collective intelligence of the users. Hence, there are three kinds of Web 2.0 platforms, which are also mentioned in the work of Högg et al. (2008), titled "Overview of Business Models for Web 2.0 Communities". As it can be seen below in Figure 2 (Högg et al., 2008), some of the platform's applications are community-based services; the others are target-oriented services. One type of Web 2.0 platform focuses on the creation of net communities. This type of platform offers users the possibility to collect and add other individuals as friends to their account (Facebook), exchange knowledge (Wikipedia) or view music and films (YouTube). Therefore, all users pursue one common aim. Another kind of platform implements community-based services as well as target-oriented services. There, applications and tools help the user to create his or her own blogs or wikis. An example of such a service with which Wikis can be created is Wetpaint. An online cooperation which implies common work on content is an example of the third kind of Web 2.0 platform. This contains strictly goal-oriented applications. Thus, several users have the possibility to work together on content on the Internet, for example, by doing online brainstorming (Högg et al., 2008, p. 49 following).

In relation to the research question of how important social media for the fashion industry is, brands will be analysed with applications with community-based services such as Facebook, Twitter and YouTube. These services offer, for companies, the best opportunity to merchandise their brands and products.

Figure 2. Clustered Overview of Web 2.0 Applications

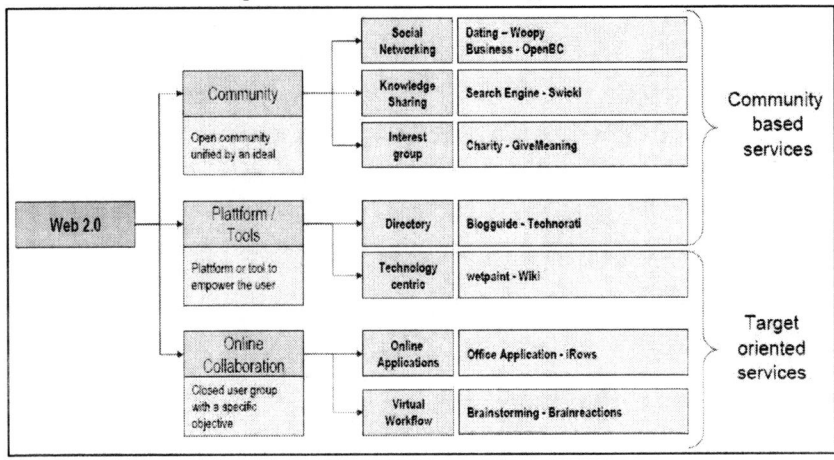

Source: Högg et al. (2008)

2.3 Marketers and Customers

The fact that Louis Vuitton got "brand-jacked" by using social media applications shows that with social media, it is not just the marketers who have the power to create a brand image. The technology of Web 2.0 empowered marketers and made it easier to reach the customers, but it has also empowered the consumers (Fournier and Avery, 2011, p. 193).

Fournier and Avery (2011) discuss this topic in their paper "The Uninvited Brand" in more depth. They analyse how web-based power struggles between marketers and consumer. Additionally they explore the emergent cultural landscape of open-source branding and explain marketing strategies in the context of social media. The first notable point they make in this context is that it is important for companies in the time of Web 2.0 and social media to listen to the users. Active listening can not

9

only prevent a negative company image but can also strengthen the company's brands and expedite them as well (Fournier and Avery, 2011, p. 197). Furthermore, marketers need to communicate with those who like their brand. It is not enough to put words in their mouth. Rather, it is more about creating things that consumers want to talk about and to submit to them the passion of the brand fitted to their needs. People love to talk, and they love using social media because they want to be heard and to gain a sense of their importance in the world (Bueno, 2007, p. 535). By creating consumer-driven programmes through which consumers can publish and share their ideas and work together with the company to build next-generation products, some companies have found a good way to communicate and include the users in their online brand activities. Hence, ceding power to the broad mass of users serves to get some power back while creating a feeling for the users that they are important to the company.

But in the end, Fournier and Avery (2011, p. 197) argue that the company still knows what is good for its brand and what is not and, in particular, what is best for the company itself. Therefore, marketers should not fully transfer the control to the customer and be slaves of influence. They risk losing the brand and a lot of money. In this case, it is also notable that the main users of social media platforms are under 25 and hence not always a brand's main target group (Riegner, 2007, p. 438). The main customers for a brand like Louis Vuitton, for example, might differ in age and online behaviour to H&M customers; due to Louis Vuitton's higher product prices. The brand's customers might exist more in the background and might have a different opinion compared to those who actively communicate on social platforms and influence each other in opinion creation. This is one of the objectives that will be researched and is necessary for defining the importance of social media. The target user group might differ between several priced labels.

The biggest influences on the diffusion process have those individuals who are experts in the respective, subject complex. These "opinion leaders" are used by the majority of individuals as sources of information in opinion formation. Katz and Lazarsfeld (1955, p. 3) define them as "the individuals who were likely to influence other persons in their immediate environment". Opinion leaders are characterised, above all, by their extensive knowledge in one field and are therefore used by other individuals as a source of information. Opinion leaders have a more intense relation to the mass media in comparison to other individuals and are deeply anchored in their subject area (Corey, 1971, p. 48). However, individuals with many connections in the form of acquaintances or friendships with other members on the network called "social hubs" have an influence as well. For companies and their marketing, the identification of such individuals is important as they show a big number of connections in the form of acquaintances or friendships on the network. Opinion leaders and social hubs influence the masses with their extensive knowledge and their highly persuasive abilities and play an important role in the introduction of innovations. If the marketing identifies these individuals, it can include them in their marketing strategies to reach the masses (Dressler and Telle, 2009, p. 167). Referring to the fashion industry, people like to engage with fashion brands and share online what they are wearing. This is first and foremost a representation of themselves and brands are often chosen to express their personality to others by using social media applications (Thenextweb.com, 2012). The fashion industry realised the major impact these people have on the success of the particular brands they engage with; due to their well developed and linked online social networks. For the 2012 Fashion Week in Paris, some famous designers like Karl Lagerfeld, invited fashion bloggers to attend at their fashion shows and were seated in the front rows (Laurent, 2012).

Additionally, according to a study by Matthew Lee (2006), the most common reason for users to join community groups and start sharing opinions about brands is for their own satisfaction and because they feel that it is their responsibility to tell others about their experiences. Those can be positive as well as negative. Fournier and Avery (2011) discovered that the two most-feared means of influence and communication in the social web for a brand, and especially for marketers, are criticism and parody. Due to the new technologies, such as blogging, ranking or rating, consumers are able to share easily and quickly their dissatisfaction and complaints. As already mentioned in the case of Louis Vuitton, brands can find

11

themselves quickly at the centre of a storm of critics with whom they must deal (Fournier and Avery, 2011, p. 200).

Brian Gilbert (2009, p. 5), vice president of integrated marketing at Hacker Group, states that criticism is the hardest part of jumping into new media but dealing with a critic well will very often earn the company a fan for life. This means that criticism is not just a danger for a brand; marketers can also use online critics to gain approval from them. Social media platforms can be used as a free marketing research tool that can save costs. Firms can gain from innovative branding opportunities (Hollenbeck, 2006, p. 484).

Schultz (2008, p. 11) expounds in his article "Actions, Not Promises—The Future Ain't Going to Be Like the Past!" that branding has to change from the tradition of non reliable promises, which marketers make, to actual in-market performance and repeatable brand experiences. He refers, especially in relation to brand experience, to his personal experience with websites, customer service and influential personalities such as blogger or broadcaster. Marketing should be a combination of pushing out traditional branding messages and responding effectively to the questions and concerns customers are raising, as mentioned earlier in this paper. But in the end, even the worst parody campaign can have some positive effects for the brand. When, for example, a parody video is seen more often than the original video, and is more talked about, the brand will stay in people's minds. Similarly, a celebrity such as Madonna gains from negative campaigns as well, because her name as a brand remains in people's minds. Marketers can also use parody to promote their products in a funny way by jumping on the bandwagon and creating their own parody advertisements and videos for the brand. At least they can learn from it and gain a free advantage.

The findings of previous works mentioned in this section are used to observe and analyse how fashion brands interact with customers by using social media applications. Therefore, these criteria build the basis of the whole research process. Observing the interactivity of different brands in Facebook, Twitter and YouTube helps determine the success of using social media and, finally, the importance of social media for the fashion industry.

2.4 Social Media Monitoring

Only a small amount of research has been done to measure the abovementioned theoretical criteria, the effectiveness of social media marketing and hence the importance of social media for companies. Most of this research states that it is difficult to measure the effectiveness of social media.

Hoffman and Fodor (2010) mention in their paper "Can You Measure the ROI of Your Social Media Marketing?" that the main reason for this difficulty lies the way marketers have measured their marketing efficiency in the past by focusing on direct sales, direct cost reductions or increases in market share from campaigns. Moreover, the authors advise to focus more on key motivation factors that a social media customer has as the online content is more user-generated rather than marketer-generated. Those factors, which are called the 4 C's, are:

- ❖ Connection
- ❖ Creation
- ❖ Consumption
- ❖ Control

In today's modern world of Web 2.0 customers are fully in control of their online experiences and want to connect online with other users to create, share and consume online content. Hence, to measure the importance of social media, it is advisable to analyse the active "investments" customers will make as they engage with the company's brands at the specific social media application, such as blog comments, registration or active participation (Hoffman and Fodor, 2010). Hoffmann and Fodor (2010) point out, that social media enhances the formation of brand awareness and brand engagement, due to an increase of word of mouth. This is how the 4 C's contribute to measure social media activity.

The paper refers to the findings of Fournier and Avery (2011) and establishes a way of measuring success for marketers using social media applications to create brand awareness or brand engagement. Nevertheless, examples of data gathering are missing as well; the second part of the paper describes paths to develop an effective social media strategy rather than continuing answering the title question of whether social media activity is measurable. Above all Hoffman and Fodor's paper provides a good basis to answer the research question about the importance of social media. Table 1. gives a short overview of the various social metrics for social media which will be helpful for the local research.

Table 1. Metrics for Social Media Applications

Social Media Applications	Brand Awareness	Brand Engagement	Word of Mouth
Blogs	• number of unique visits • number of return visits • number of time bookmarked • search ranking	• number of members • number of RSS feed subscribers • number of comments • amount of user-generated content • average length of time on site • number of responses to polls, contests, surveys	• number of references to blog in other media (online/offline) • number of reblogs • number of times badge displayed on other sites • number of "likes"
Microblogging (e.g., Twitter)	• number of tweets about the brand • valence of tweets +/- • number of followers	• number of followers • number of replies	• number of retweets
Social Networks (e.g., Facebook)	• number of members/fans • number of installs of applications • number of impressions • number of bookmarks • number of reviews/ratings and valance +/-	• number of comments • number of active users • number of "likes" • number of user-generated items (photos, threads, replies) • usage metrics of applications/widgets • impressions-to-interactions ratio • rate of activity (how often members personalize profiles, bios, links, etc.)	• frequency of appearances in timeline of friends • number of posts on wall • number of reposts/shares • number of responses to friend referral invites
Video / Photosharing (e.g., YouTube)	• number of views of video/photo • valence of video/photo rating +/-	• number of replies • number of page views • number of comments • number of subscribers	• number of embeddings • number of incoming links • number of references in mock-ups or derived work • number of times republished in other social media and offline • number of "likes"

Source: Hoffman and Fodor (2010)

Previous quantitative research about the social media strategies of fashion labels, like Hoffmann and Fodor's (2010) or Uitz's (2012) refer to the tools listed in the table to analyse how the labels interact via the top three social media applications: Facebook, Twitter and YouTube (see Baltner, 2011). Data is collected by counting, for example, the numbers of fans (Facebook), the number of tweets about the brand (Twitter) and the number of views of a video (YouTube).

Furthermore, the researchers compare the different labels in relation to these facts and evaluate a social media strategy for each of the labels. It is a good example of how data will be collected and analysed during the research process of this study. To answer the research question, this model of measuring the impact of social media is helpful and the research process will be based on it. However, it is not necessary to find or formulate one or more social media strategies for the labels to answer the question of importance.

The previously performed research seems to be, in some ways, a bit superficial and not developed enough. The evaluation is not as extended as it could be. For example, other key terms about social media interactivity, such as a brand's blog or social bookmarking, could be included. Dowling and Weeks (2011), for example, define three different kinds of analysis in their paper, "Media analysis: What Is It Worth?". They describe the roles of:

1. Salience and sentiment analysis;
2. Theme and contradiction analysis; and
3. Problem and solution analysis.

Each of those three types provides a different media profile for an organisation, and all three types should be part of the organisation's research. All three together profile the image of an organisation in the media. The salience and sentiment analysis is described as the measurement of the stories and language used by the customer published, in this case, at social media platforms to describe the brand or the organisation. Theme and contradiction analysis is about clustering the given comments on the social media platforms in different themes. Finally, problem and solution analysis is used to understand a particular problem to save costs or protect revenues. Using different case studies, the authors explain the three kinds of analyses, and the value of the media analysis is listed at the end of the paper for each case study. The findings in this paper support, with a few points, the way the research for the importance of social media should be structured. For example, the authors mention that key opinion leaders should be identified at the beginning. It must be noted that the research Dowling and Weeks performed, and hence their different analyses, measure only the image of a brand or company at the social media platforms or other media. However, this can be helpful to explain the impact of social media to define the question of who owns the influence in the social web—marketers or customers.

Additionally, based on the tools Hoffman and Fodor (2012) refer to for the measurement of social media activity, the analytic social media company, called Socialbakers (2012c), developed two formulas to calculate a company's online average engagement rate and response rate. This helps to determine a company's social media activity in a more analytical, quantitative way in relation to brand awareness and brand engagement. Whereas, the measurement method of Hoffmann and Fodor (2012) is mainly based on qualitative (non-numerical) objectives (Uitz, 2012). Furthermore, by using these formulas a company is able to compare the engagement rate and response rate of different brands they own and hence making conclusions about successful social media strategies. Social media manager can measure the brands' performances and decide what it is really worth acting upon and which type of posts are more effective ones in terms of engaging more users (Socialbakers, 2012c). Figure 2.1 shows the two formulas developed by Socialbakers (2012c).

Figure 2.1 Socialbakers Formulas

$$Engagement\ Rate = \frac{\dfrac{Likes + Comments + Shares}{\#\ of\ Wall\ Posts\ made\ by\ page}}{Total\ Fans} * 100$$

$$Response\ Rate = \frac{Comments + Likes + Shares}{Total\ Fans} * 100$$

Source: Socialbakers (2012c)

But there are limitations coming up with these two formulas. Wisemetrics (2012) analyzes in their online article "Why The Current Facebook Engagement Rate Calculation Is Inaccurate" the engagement rate formula, set up by Socialbakers (2012c) and explains the weaknesses of using this formula, what it describes and how to interpret the values. At the end the author comes up with an alternative formula, which is described as more "significant and useful". Due to the fact that the engagement rate measures, how well fans and followers interact with the shared content, the author mainly criticize that exactly this is not fulfilled by the formula (Wisemetrics, 2012). Five issues are determined in the publication by Wisemetrics (2012) which question the reliability of the formula.

At first, the author states, that the formula does not include all interactions. It only measures likes, comments and shares and misses out the video, links and photo clicks made by fans on Facebook, Twitter or Youtube. This does not include a missing of the actual number of users who viewed these media posts (Naidu, 2012). Within the fashion industry these kinds of posts are important to measure as a lot of created content are based on media links and include photos or videos (Wisemetrics, 2012). This leads to the second issue the author is clarifying. The formula is based on the number of fans only; instead of measuring the number of actual users reached. The most shared content is not only seen by fans and followers, moreover by their friends. Lately, it is more important to include the number of users reached instead of the number of fans as statistically 84% of a company's Facebook fans, for example, do not view the created content (Wisemetrics, 2012). Hence a page with less overall interactions but with more shares and with a wider friends network may outperform another page with way more fans or more interactions, when it comes to number of users reached (Wisemetrics, 2012). The third issue concerns the fact that the formula derives a ratio of the total number of likes, comments and shares made by fans and non-fans, from the total number of fans which creates a bias suggesting a bigger engagement rate. All likes, comments and shares made by non-fans would need to be excluded (Naidu, 2012). The fourth point cannot be seen as a significant statement against the use of the formula as the author just mentions that with more posts the

17

engagement rate can be increased. This is a clear fact which should not to be criticized as an issue. Companies need to increase their engagement rate by posting more. The more they post the more fans will like their pages and share the content. The last issue includes that the formula only measures interactions but not the actual proportion of fans who interact on the social media platforms. Therefore, the fact that one fan can make several likes or comments per day is not considered in the formula.

By the new formula the author makes clear, that the above mentioned issues will be suspended. Additionally, the credibility and accuracy are higher than the formula developed by Socialbakers (2012c). The general formula Wisemetrics (2012) suggests to conduct divides the number of engaged users by the number of users reached, multiplied by 100. In case a company is interested in calculating an engagement rate benchmark between several pages, the author advises to divide the number of engaged users by the number of made posts, this needs to be divided by the number of users reached and multiplied by 100. Figure 2.2 shows the developed formulas by Wisemetrics (2012).

Figure 2.2 Wisemetrics Formulas

$$Engagement\ Rate\ = \frac{Engaged\ Users}{Reached\ Users} * 100$$

or

$$Engagement\ Rate\ = \frac{\frac{Engaged\ Users}{\#\ of\ posts}}{Reached\ Users} * 100$$

Source: Wisemetrics (2012)

However, neither Wisemetrics (2012) nor Socialbakers (2012c) divine in their publications what the calculated value predicates and how to interpret these. Expected are results in percentage between 0 and 1 for Socialbakers' formulas and results above 1 for Wisemetrics' formulas. Hence it is unclear, if a higher calculated value close to 1 is more desirable or a lower value, which is closer to 0. Both do not consider any limitations of their research in their publications. Therefore, the researcher included all formulas in this study's research process to test these formulas for credibility, to make decisions which formula is the most useful to measure social media activity, to analyse the collected data and hence to compare the different brands' performances on the several social media platforms.

The previous section discussed the review of relevant literature and findings in regards to the importance of social media for the fashion industry. It has shown that there are many ways of using Web 2.0 and that the new technology has permitted the rise of social networking where the research will be addressed. One way to answer the research question will be to determine who owns the influence, because there are power struggles between marketers and customers. Furthermore, examples of previous researches were given to analyse their effectiveness to get impressions of how a company's social media activity can be measured. As already mentioned at the beginning of this chapter, an exact definition of the term "Brand" will be given in chapter 4, together with an explanation of brand awareness and brand engagement.

3 Methodology

3.1 Introduction

This chapter provides information about the methodological approach of the study, the research design, including the research strategy and the empirical techniques. Furthermore, to ensure that the gathered data was credible and valid, the research process is described as well as the methods of data collection, data analysis and the design of questionnaires and interviews. Limitations according to this study are described at the end of this chapter.

The main purpose of this study is to estimate the importance of social media use for the fashion industry. For the investigation of this study's purpose and hence for the fulfilment of the associated objectives, listed in chapter 1, an analytical research approach was developed including an online observation of 12 international fashion labels, user questionnaires and interviews with marketers.

Based on previous literature, it is helpful to clarify the used terminology and to distinguish between the terms "research methodology" and "research methods" first. Jankowicz (2005) describes for example the term "methodology" as the analysis of, and rationale for, the particular method or methods used in a given study, and in that type of study in general. Saunders et al (2009) defines "research methods" as the techniques and the procedures used to analyse data, whereas, "research methodology" is the theory of how research should be undertaken.

3.2 Research Design and Strategy

The nature of this study refers to a multiphase research design which involves multiple phases of data collection and analysis. This allows a greater diversity of views to be reflected in the study and helps to explain relationships between the variables. Furthermore, multiphase research helps to prove the credibility of the study to establish a generalisability at the end (Saunders et al., 2012). This research consists of three multiple phases and starts with a quantitative research approach, which is based on numerical data from a structured observation process. This phase is followed by another quantitative approach in form of questionnaires and then by a phase of qualitative data collection. The qualitative research part is set up as a non-numerical approach and consists of interviews. Therefore, the study's prioritisation is based on a quantitative research approach. Qualitative data is mainly used to explain particular findings further and to support the findings of the quantitative research.

A research survey was conducted for the data collection through the use of user questionnaires, structured marketer interviews and a structured online observation of 12 fashion brands. By using a survey strategy, quantitative data can be analysed quantitatively using descriptive statistics. The collected data can be used to suggest possible reasons for particular relationships between variables and finally to produce models of these relationships (Saunders et al., 2012).

3.3 Data Collection

For the data collection of this study, both types of sources were used to guarantee the highest amount of reliability, validity and credibility of the study.

1. Secondary sources
2. Primary sources

Mooi and Sarstedt (2011, p. 29) define secondary data as data that has already been collected by other researchers for a different purpose. This data will be used by summarising the already existing findings from past studies to provide additional or different knowledge and help to formulate conclusions. The use of primary data includes self conducted research by the responsible researcher to collect the data that did not exist before. The collection of each kind of data from the two sources will be explained in the following for this study.

3.3.1 Secondary Data

According to Saunders et al. (2003), secondary data includes quantitative as well as qualitative data. For this study, the secondary data was collected from secondary sources, such as Business Source Premier, Science Direct, ProQuest and Mintel. This data is qualitative (non-numerical) and mainly based on articles from Fournier and Avery (2011), Hoffman and Fodor (2010) and Socialbakers (2012c). The considered secondary sources are used to

- clarify issues related to social media and the fashion industry
- be aware of social media weaknesses
- discuss different kinds of social media measurement methods
- develop a strategy to solve problems in measuring social media activity
- inform about current challenges marketers have to deal with when using social media

These topics have been discussed earlier in the literature review chapter. The viewed secondary literature helped the researcher to clarify the research question and the research focus. It makes the primary data collection more specific as it identifies issues and deficiencies as well as what additional information needs to be collected (Managementguide, 2012). Furthermore, it indicated upcoming difficulties in the primary research which the researcher has to consider before designing the primary research process. Due to the currency of the research topic associated with social media and fashion, there are restricted sources available. Most sources are online and available in the form of online journals, rather than in books. Not much research has been done in the past, in terms of social media and the fashion industry. The validity and reliability of the information provided by these sources have been critically evaluated by the researcher to ensure the quality of the study.

3.3.2 Primary Data

After critically reviewing the secondary literature, the primary data collection process was designed according to the findings from these sources. Due to the few published studies and available data on social media, it was necessary to collect data on a primary base to develop a solid strategy and to answer the research question. According to Ghauri and Gronhaug (2005), data collected on a primary research approach is more consistent with the study's objectives and research question than data which was already collected by another researcher with a different study purpose. In addition, the use of primary data allows the researcher a higher level of control over how the information is collected. Decisions can be made about the study's sample size (e.g. how many responses), the location of the research (e.g. geographical area) and time frames (Knowthis.com, 2012).

To collect this study's primary data, three main methods have been used within an overall time frame of three months. Structured observations (quantitative data), structured questionnaires (quantitative data) and structured interviews (qualitative data) were set up to answer the research question. These three methods will be explained in more detail below, together with the purpose of each method and the process of data collection.

Structured Observations

The main part of the primary research is based on the observations of 12 fashion labels and their activity on social media platforms. During a one month observation period in July 2012, 12 fashion companies where observed on a daily basis. Every day, the interactivity of each label was counted and researched from today's three main social media platforms: Facebook, Twitter and YouTube. Those platforms have the highest user traffic at the time of this study (cf. McCarthy, 2012).

All types of platforms are social media applications but differ in their goal functionalities. Facebook belongs to a group of social network applications, Twitter is a microblogging platform and YouTube is a video- and photosharing application (see Table 1. in chapter 2). Currently, there are 30,595,980 Facebook users in the United Kingdom, by which 7,648,995 are between 25 and 34 years of age (Socialbakers, 2012b). In addition, the 12 fashion labels were chosen from three different price genres (low-, medium- and high-priced labels); respectively the four most successful in each genre. The low-priced section includes brands like H&M, Topshop, Zara and Pull&Bear. Whereas brands like Massimo Dutti, Hollister, COS and REISS are listed as medium-priced labels. The luxury section includes brands like Hugo Boss, Gucci, Louis Vuitton and Burberry. All are operating on an international

Figure 3.1 Observed Fashion Brands

level. Figure 3.1 gives an overview of the observed brands. By observing brands from different price genres on several, (not only one specific social media platform) existing differences in the brand's social media activities of the particular genres could be outlined and conclusions made such as which kind of platform is the most profitable in terms of brand awareness and brand engagement. The online activity of each brand was measured by daily counting and collecting the number of posts a brand made, the number of likes, comments and shares made by the user to each post, the number of brand replies to user comments or questions and finally, the number of fans (Facebook), followers (Twitter) and subscribers (YouTube). Furthermore, to guarantee better analysis and recommendations at the end of the study the number of user-generated items such as photos or videos were also counted as well as noting the content of the posts. Table 2. gives a short overview on the kinds of variables from each of the platforms.

After successfully collecting the data, the findings were checked for possible errors before they were analysed within a three steps process. The gathered quantitative data from the structured online observations of the twelve fashion brands were viewed, processed and analysed. Quantitative analysis techniques, such as graphs, charts or statistics were used to transfer the data from their raw form into meaningful information.

Table 2. Social Media Platform Variables

Facebook	Twitter	YouTube
• Number of fans	• Number of follower	• Number of subscribers
• Number of posts by brand	• Number of tweets by brand	• Number of posts by brand
• Number of replies by brand	• Number of replies by brand	• Number of views by user
• Number of Illustrations	• Number of retweets by user	• Number of likes by user
• Number of likes by users	• Number of comments by user	• Number of dislikes by user
• Number of comments by user	• Kind of tweets	• Number of comments by user
• Number of shares by user		
• Kind of posts		

These techniques helped the researcher to explore, present, describe and examine relationships and trends within the data (Saunders et al., 2012). Diagrams were mainly used to present the frequency of occurrence, whereas formulas were used to establish statistical relationships between the variables.

After successfully collecting the data, the findings were checked for possible errors before they were analysed within a three steps process. The gathered quantitative data from the structured online observations of the twelve fashion brands were viewed, processed and analysed. Quantitative analysis techniques, such as graphs, charts or statistics were used to transfer the data from their raw form into meaningful information. These techniques helped the researcher to explore, present, describe and examine relationships and trends within the data (Saunders et al., 2012). Diagrams were mainly used to present the frequency of occurrence, whereas formulas were used to establish statistical relationships between the variables.

For example, bar charts and multiple bar charts outline the volume of posts made by the fashion brands per month. One bar illustrates the amount of posts made by one company. The higher the amount, the higher the particular bar. Thus, brands can be ranked from the most active brand using the specific social media application to the least active brand. Pie charts reflect in this stage of the analysis process the users' engagement measured in daily likes, comments and shares. All daily collected data was added up to one month to make it easier to compare. Additionally, tables were used to outline the top three fastest growing fashion brands for each social media platform. This was measured by the number of friends, followers and subscribers at the beginning of the observation process and at the end. Statements can be given if a higher activity rate on social media platforms leads automatically to more followers.

Three existing formulas from secondary literature were proved to calculate the brands' average engagement rates and their average response rates to find a reliable way companies can measure their social media activity and hence make decisions about their investment in social media. The original formulas set up by Socialbakers (2012c) and Wisemetrics (2012) were discussed in more detail in the Literature Review of this study (chapter 2). All formulas were slightly modified by the researcher for the several social media applications. An example of the formulas used to calculate the average engagement and response rate on Facebook is given below in Figure 3.2. A complete list of all used formulas is attached in the Appendix (Appedix D). Furthermore, the exact validity of both formulas will be determined in the discussion section of chapter 5.

Figure 3.2 Formulas Engagement Rate & Response Rate

$$Engagement\ Rate_{Socialbakers} = \frac{\frac{Likes + Comments + Shares}{\#\ of\ Wall\ Posts\ made\ by\ page}}{Total\ Fans} \times 100$$

$$Response\ Rate_{Socialbakers} = \frac{Comments + Likes + Shares}{Total\ Fans} \times 100$$

$$Engagement\ Rate_{Wisemetrics} = \frac{\frac{Users\ Engaged}{\#\ of\ Posts\ made\ by\ channel}}{Users\ Reached} \times 100 = \frac{\frac{Comments + Likes + Dislikes}{\#\ of\ Posts\ made\ by\ channel}}{Total\ Views} \times 100$$

Sources: Socialbakers (2012c); Wisemetrics (2012)

Structured Questionnaires

After successfully collecting the data from the observations, an electronic online questionnaire was created to support the findings from the observations and to test their validity and credibility. Furthermore, to find out how the individual consumer engages with fashion brands when using social media. 50 internet users were contacted by Facebook and Twitter. This self-completion questionnaire consists of ten questions concerning their usage of social media applications and their behaviour on social media platforms which respondents completed by themselves in their own time. The questionnaire was written in English. General questions about "Gender" and "Age" of the users where not considered as these have already been researched in other studies and were not necessary for the purpose of this study. The complete questionnaire is attached in the Appendix (Appedix B). A questionnaire strategy was chosen for this purpose of the study as respondents are able to complete the questionnaire in their own time at home and are able to think about the questions in more depth. This makes the results of the questionnaire more credible. By using an online questionnaire it is easier to reach people from different geographical areas and a large number of people can be contacted at low cost in a short time (Kirklees, 2012). The questionnaire was designed for a quantitative purpose; to collect numerical data. Its planning and development process includes five different stages.

The first stage is about initial considerations. Here it is important to determine the target group which will be contacted and to clarify the type of the collected information (Kirklees, 2012). For this research the questionnaire was designed for a quantitative approach and any kind of internet user without any limitations on age and gender as this is not decisive for the research purpose. Furthermore, decisions were made at this stage of the process about the method of administering the questionnaire and finally, how the findings will be analysed at the end as this effects the design of the questionnaire right from the beginning.

The second stage the researcher went through in developing the questionnaire relates to the questions themselves. The researcher has to make sure that each question adds value, is clear and easy to understand without creating any kind of confusion for the respondents. This is followed by a stage of sorting the questions into a logical order, where similar themed questions are grouped together. Therefore, more simple and general questions are placed right at the beginning of the questionnaire before asking more specific questions. This makes it easier for the respondents to answer the questionnaire. A confidentially agreement was created to guarantee that personal details are not disclosed to third parties and are used for

27

research purposes only, and that any data used in the report will not be linked to any respondents. Before issuing the final questionnaire in the last stage, a pilot questionnaire was given to five people for a pre-test. This enables the researcher to prove people's ability to answer the questions, highlights areas of confusion and points errors out. After pre-testing the draft questionnaires the final ones were sent out in the last stage. To maximise the response rate a reminder was sent out three times per day in intervals of two days. Furthermore, respondents being informed about the quantity of questions and the amount of time. To lower the rate of drop-outs, a short introductory letter was attached to the questionnaire. Figure 3.3 presents the different stages the researcher went through in developing the questionnaire.

Figure 3.3 Questionnaire Design

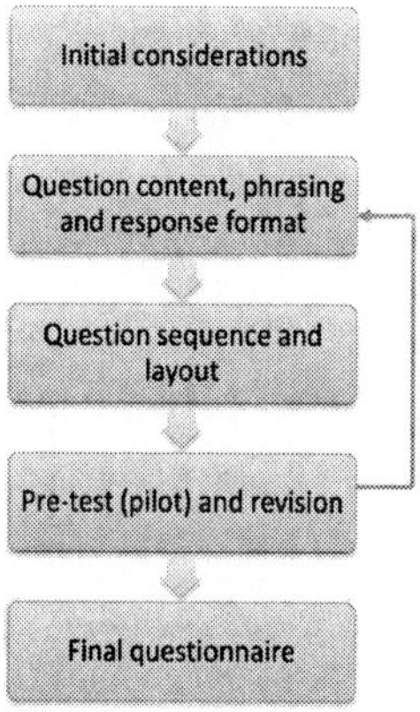

Source: Kirklees, 2012

The quantitative results of the user questionnaire are represented by bar charts, pie charts and multiple line graphs. Bar charts mainly show the frequency of occurrences of the different categories the user could choose in their answer. Whether pie charts are used to demonstrate the proportion of occurrences of an answer category. Multiple line graphs show the trends of the variables included in one question (Saunders et al., 2012).

The researcher was aware of the fact that response rates can be low, as well as control over who completes an online questionnaire is restricted and can lead to bias in the research. Furthermore, limitations exist as the questionnaire is inappropriate for people with reading difficulties or visual impairments and those who do not read English (Kirklees 2012). All participants were included on a voluntary basis without any element of force, fraud, duress, over-reaching, or other form of coercion by the researcher. No names, personal information of users or participants, neither any information that go against regulation rights (cf. Mrs.org.uk, 2012) were used in this research. The researcher was, during the complete research process, aware of these legal and ethical issues. Possible upcoming problems which could affect the research were also considered by the researcher. Difficulties could have arisen in terms of the technology used. Due to the fact that the research is based on social media applications (Facebook, Twitter, YouTube) it was necessary that those applications are still providing their services during the time that the research was running. Such technical problems could have lead to interruptions of the research process. Further supplementary social media platforms would need to be considered in the research, such as LinkedIn instead of Facebook, or Vimeo as an alternative to YouTube. As well as access to the internet was a basic requirement for this research as it was the main medium used to conduct the research process. Therefore it was also necessary that the participants of the research were provided with access to the internet.

Structured Interviews

The third part of the survey strategy and final stage of the complete research process includes structured interviews with marketers. Five marketing and social media manager, all related to the fashion industry, were contacted for a face-to-face interview on a one to one basis. The marketers are based in the United Kingdom and Germany. This qualitative form of research enables the interviewer the use of different data collection techniques, such as open ended questions (Advaithinfoserv.com, 2012). These are used for the purpose of this research. More information can be gathered as the interviewed people tend to share more information when someone is asking questions. Furthermore, it is easier to ask a follow up question and get examples of the content people are talking about (Thenonprofittimes.com, 2012). By using face-to-face interviews, respondents cannot skip questions as they are led through each question by the researcher. But, in comparison to online questionnaires, structured interviews are more time intensive as the researcher has to make appropriate appointments with the respondents and attend to these (Advaithinfoserv.com, 2012). According to the design of the interviews, the researcher went through the same process as mentioned in the section before for designing the questionnaire. Eleven questions were asked, beginning with general questions and ending with open ended questions. The interviews were audio-recorded and subsequently notes were made by the researcher during the interviews. A confidentiality agreement was included as well to guarantee that personal details and information about the company are not disclosed to third parties and used for research purposes only. Participants were provided with an interim summary of the progress which outlines the study's purpose; objectives; the findings and conclusions to date; the level of confidence in these and the reasons for holding the interviews.

The face-to-face interviews help to clarify the question of how fashion companies are using social media and what the main purpose is. It was necessary to find out if marketers are aware of the impact social media can have on their brands and especially if they are conscious about difficulties or advantages related to the use of social media. This was done by including some similar questions from the user questionnaire in the interviews. A comparison of the given answers to these questions enabled the researcher to find differences or similarities among the users' social media behavior and the marketers' awareness of this behavior. As the interviews relate to the findings of the structured observations as well as the online questionnaire they were designed and held after analysing the results of these previous two research stages. The interview questions can be viewed in the Appendix of this paper (Appendix C). The qualitative interviews with the marketers were analysed by viewing each question separately. The answers to each question were compared with each other and summarised. Audio-records of the interviews were compared with the notes, the researcher took during the interviews. Furthermore, the researcher paid attention to the participant's non-verbal communications and to the tone in which answers were given.

Limitations existed concerning time and date to held the interviews, which were set by the marketers. This affected the further development and completion of the study. The researcher has had to manage delays which occurred due to that issue. Furthermore, the given answers by the interviewees might not be representative as they might not relate to the interviewer's questions. The use of secondary data included some limitations in collecting and measuring the data. No reliable research has ever been done before in this new social media environment. Hence, there was no overall, useable method to collect data and perform the analysis. The quantity of the collected data during the observation process could have been insufficient to form a significant statement to the research purpose.

At the end, all analysed data was compared to each other to formulate an overall conclusion of the findings. During the complete analysis process, the researcher was always aware of the formulated research question and the study's objectives. The results will be presented and discussed in chapter 5.

4. The Fashion Industry and their Brand Engagement

4.1 Introduction

This chapter lists, categorises and describes the twelve observed fashion brands in this study. The brands are separated into three different price genres (luxury labels, medium priced labels and low priced labels). Company details are given as well as information about the conducted social media applications of each brand. The chapter begins with a short definition of the term "Brand" and explains this in the context of brand awareness and brand engagement. At the end a summary is provided with an overview of all the key facts about the involved brands.

4.2 Definition Brand

The Oxford American Dictionary (1980) defines the word "brand" as follows:

> Brand (noun): a trade mark, goods of a particular
> make: a mark of identification made with a hot iron,
> the iron used for this: a piece of burning or charred
> wood, (verb): to mark with a hot iron, or to label
> with a trade mark.

Furthermore, a brand can be a name, term, sign, symbol, or design, or a combination of these; which is intended to identify the goods or services of one seller or group of sellers and to differentiate them from those of competitors (Levy, 1958). It is also a specific type of product manufactured by a particular company under a particular name (Oxforddictionaries.com, 2012). In a modern business and marketing related definition, each brand is a set of concepts and images that represent a company, product or service. It is the essence or promise of what will be delivered. Consumers refer to a brand as a logo, tag line or audio jingle. Brands enable them to easily identify the offerings of a particular company. A brand can be an umbrella under which different products can be offered and used to generate economic leverage and strategic advantage by creating awareness of their product portfolio (Persuasivebrands.com, 2012).

In this context, brand awareness is the extent to which a brand is recognized by potential customers, and associated with a particular product. Creating and enhancing brand awareness is the primary goal of advertising (Businessdictionary.com, 2012b). The interactive process of generating awareness for a particular brand is called brand engagement. This includes the engagement of customers, advancing them into new creative realms or markets, where they can add value to the brand and competitors cannot follow. As mentioned in chapter 2 social media has become a popular marketing tool to generate brand awareness. Customers can be forwarded into an interactive process of brand engagement to develop a stronger sense of self (Tenayagroup.com, 2009).

According to this study the twelve observed fashion brands are classified by three different price genres (low, medium and premium) and are explained in more detail in the following.

4.3 Premium Priced Labels

Premium priced, luxury brands which offer high class quality products are defined by Heine (2012) as a symbol of "the best from the best for the best". These brands are regarded as images in the minds of consumers. They are associated with high level of price, quality, aesthetics, rarity, extraordinariness and their core products (Heine, 2012). Luxury goods are in general purchased by individuals who have a higher disposable income or wealth than the average consumers (Businessdictionary.com, 2012a). For this study the four luxury brands Hugo Boss, Burberry, Louis Vuitton and Gucci were observed.

Hugo Boss

Hugo Boss is a German based luxury brand for high-end women's and men's fashion since 1924. The company employs a workforce of 10,000 people. In the fiscal year 2010, Hugo Boss generated an annual sales of EUR 1.7 billion. It is among the world's most profitable apparel manufacturers. The company's product portfolio includes the classical core brand BOSS and the casual brand HUGO. The brand's product range includes classic-modern business wear, elegant evening, relaxed casual fashion, shoes and leather accessories, as well as fragrances, eyewear, watches, children's fashion and motorcycle helmets. Through the diversity in the brand, Hugo Boss creates a product differentiation and targets different kinds of consumer groups. Customers can find their products all over the world in 124 countries with more than 6,100 points of sales. The stores are mostly operated by franchise partners and by the company itself. The company invests mainly in marketing activities such as print advertising and sponsorship of cultural and sport events (Hugoboss, 2012). This enhances the worldwide recognition and image of the brand. The company clearly states that the use of social media became an important factor in the company's marketing strategy alongside the traditional advertising. Todays relevant target groups are mainly targeted by these new marketing instruments such as social networks. Hugo Boss includes the three main social media applications Facebook, Twitter and Youtube in their marketing strategy but also uses applications like Google+, Foresquare, Instagram, Pinterest and a mobile phone app to engage with customers (Hugoboss, 2012).

Burberry

Burberrry is a British luxury brand, founded in 1856. Since this time the brand has become defined by its outerwear heritage and its iconic trench coat. By the time founder Thomas Burberry invented gabardine, the brand became synonymous with adventurers and aviators who wore his coats. Burberry's distinctive tartan pattern has become one of the most popular and well known trademarks. Today the company's main focus lies in distributing clothing and fashion accessories and licensing fragrances. Customers can find branded stores and franchises around the world, and also can buy Burberry products at third-party stores. Due to marketing innovations set in their current business strategy Burberry extended its reach and leverages its brand content to engage and connect consumers globally. In 2011/12, Burberry was named the fourth-fastest growing brand by Interbrand, the world's leading brand consultancy (Burberry, 2012a; Interbrand, 2012). The brand states in its strategic report, they are continuously advancing its leading position on social media in the luxury sector. From 2011 to 2012 the brand doubled its Facebook fans and YouTube views, and tripled its followers on Twitter. By adding a social media site called 'Art of The Trench' to their website, site visits could be increased by more than 60%. Furthermore an application called Tweetwalk was launched in partnership with Twitter to enable followers to see photos of the new collections first, before they went down the runway. Chinese social media platforms were considered and brand content was further leveraged for this country (Burberry, 2012a). Therefore the brand included social media applications such as Facebook, Twitter, Youtube, Instagram and Pinterest in their strategic plan.

Louis Vuitton

The tradition based brand Louis Vuitton is a French high class fashion enterprise, where high quality and luxury are the key focus. In 1987 the brand became a subsidiary of the world's leading luxury goods group LVMH Moët Hennessy - Louis Vuitton and is operating today internationally (Louisvuitton-hr.com, 2012). The group includes five different sectors in their company portfolio: Wines & Spirits, Fashion & Leather Goods, Perfumes & Cosmetics, Watches & Jewelry and Selective retailing (LVMH, 2012). Almost 100,000 people are working for LVMH whereas 18 000 people work at Louis Vuitton. Worldwide Louis Vuitton has 460 stores in 60 different countries (Louisvuitton, 2012). The brand enjoys a worldwide well known standard through its exclusive handbags which became a status symbol for women and men. Besides their interactive website louisvuitton.com the company has three social media presences at Facebook, Twitter and Youtube (Louisvuitton, 2012).

Gucci

Gucci is an Italian luxury fashion brand which designs, manufactures and sells leather goods (handbags and luggage), shoes, scarves, eyewear, perfume and jewelry. The brand was founded in 1921 in Florence, Italy and belongs today to the multibrand luxury goods company Gucci Group N.V; which owns other brands such as Yves Saint Laurent, Stella McCartney and Alexander McQueen (Linkedin, 2012;

Reuters, 2012). The brand's worldwide distribution network includes directly operated boutiques and franchised stores. Compared with the brands like Hugo Boss or Burberry, the company does not give further information to the public about their current business strategies or use of social media for their marketing activities. The brand's webpage is linked with their Facebook and Twitter page. A presence on the Youtube platform does also exist but is not linked to the main homepage (Reuters, 2012).

4.4 Medium Priced Labels

Medium or moderate priced brands lie in-between luxury brands and low priced brands. They offer products at affordable prices which are still higher than low priced products but not as high as luxury goods. The quality seems in most cases to be better than those of the lower priced products (Collinsdictionary.com, 2012). The chosen medium priced brands for this research are Reiss, Massimo Dutti, COS and Hollister.

Reiss

The brand Reiss was founded in 1971 by David Reiss in London. The first store was focused on selling men's suits and became known for its excellent tailoring. Today, the British brand includes menswear, womenswear and accessories in their portfolio and operate on an international market. In 2007 the brand launched its fully-transactional website reiss.com. During the research process of this study an increase of the brand's social media awareness was recognized on their website. Reiss started to include more social media applications and linked them with their website. The brand is now present at Facebook, Twitter, Youtube, Pinterest, Tumblr and Google+. Reiss is one of the higher priced medium labels and could as well be classified in the high priced section. According to their level of awareness in comparison to the other luxury brands and products they offer, the researcher decided to classify the brand into the upper medium priced section (Reiss, 2012).

Massimo Dutti

Massimo Dutti was founded in 1985. The Spanish company, Inditex, which owns other brands like Zara and Pull&Bear acquired the brand Massimo Dutti in 1991. At its beginnings the brand was only aimed at men's fashion. Women's fashion was launched in 1992 and includes all dimensions of styles; from urban lines to casual and formal looks. In 2003 Massimo Dutti included a children's fashion range and accessories in their product portfolio. Furthermore in the stores they offer a personal tailoring service to their customers. The brand has today over 525 stores in more than 50 countries and over 4,000 employees. An increase in social media awareness was noticeable during the research process. At the beginning of the observations the three main social media applications Facebook, Twitter and Youtube were the only ones used by the brand. The picture sharing platform Pinterest and the blogging page Tumblr were added during the observation process (Massimodutti, 2012).

COS

The Swedish fashion brand COS stands for "Collection Of Style" and belongs to the H&M Hennes & Mauritz Group. The brand includes products for men and women and stands for a good quality fashion label with affordable prices. It is well known due to its timeless design for clothing, which is a mix of classic and modern. Since the brand's launch in 2007, COS has opened stores in Europe, Asia and the Middle East. Today the brand has over 50 stores in these regions. According to its social media presence, COS has beside the main website cosstores.com, only a presence at Facebook and Youtube (Cosstores, 2012).

Hollister

The US fashion brand Hollister is one of Britain's fastest growing retail chains. The brand was founded in 2000 and is a sister chain of the US clothing group Abercrombie&Fitch. Today, it has stores all over the world and created a recognizable brand image about surfing, beach, youth and sports. The brand name and the branding date 1922 refer back to John Hollister senior who was an adventurous traveller and water sports fan during the 1920s in California (USA). By using these initials the brand created a fictitious history to communicate a cultural myth and a brand image consumers can easily engage with (BBC, 2009). Therefore no historical information about the brand is given on their website Hollisterco.com. Hollister uses Facebook and Twitter to engage with their fans.

4.5 Low Priced Labels

Low priced fashion brands are also known as mass market brands. In general these are brands that sell affordably priced products which are bought by a wide range of consumers. Low priced fashion brands are not necessarily known for selling high-quality and durable clothes or for offering an exclusive customer service. Nevertheless, these brands do meet consumers' expectations, needs and wants at reasonable prices (Investopedia.com, 2012). For this study's purpose the four fashion brands H&M, Zara, Topshop and Pull&Bear were chosen.

H&M

The other Swedish brand which is included in this survey's observation process and owned by the Hennes & Mauritz Group is H&M. The brand belongs due to its mass production of fashion clothes to the lower priced fashion labels on the market. The first store opened in 1979 in Sweden and has now over 2,600 stores with 94,000 employees all over the world. H&M's main market is Germany, followed by the US and France. In some countries customers are able to use the brand's online store to purchase their products. Thereby the customers can choose between menswear fashion, womenswear, youth and children clothing as well as cosmetics, accessories and home textile products. Social media plays an important role in the company's marketing strategy. H&M itself states that they are part of their customers daily lives due to the use of social media applications such Facebook, Twitter, Youtube, Instagram and Google+. Furthermore the brand guarantees on their website hm.com to continuously develop their strong social media presence and invite consumers to engage with the brand via social media for any requests they have (H&M, 2012).

Zara

Another brand of the Spanish Inditex group is Zara. The first store opened in 1975 in A Coruña, Spain (inditex.com, 2012). Today there are approximately over 1,444 Zara stores in 74 countries with 25,000 employees worldwide; selling menswear, womenswear, kidswear, accessories and home textiles (Inditex, 2012). Like H&M, Zara sells products at low prices, with daily new styles in stores (Manning-Schaffel, 2012). To engage online with customers the brand uses Facebook, Youtube and a mobile phone application. Zara has no Twitter account to engage with people.

Topshop

The female fashion brand Topshop, established in 1964, is part of the Arcadia Group, a UK-based clothing retailer with more than 2,500 outlets (Datamonitor, 2011). The brand operates worldwide and sells their products in more than 100 countries (Topshop, 2012). Topshop's webpage topshop.com is the beating heart of the brand's internet presence. It offers a lot of possibilities a costumer can interact with. The main purpose of the site is to sell products. This is managed by the implementation of an online store. Furthermore the website is pushing out content by integrating blog links, e-mail links for newsletters, offers and updates as well as links to the brand's social network pages (Facebook, Twitter, Tumblr, etc). Customers can discover the whole brand image and can go on a journey through the world of Topshop (Achenbach, 2012b). The brand runs its own online blog called "Inside-Out" and uses social media applications like Facebook, Twitter, Youtube, Pinterest, Tumblr, Instagram and Google+.

Pull&Bear

Belonging to the Spanish Inditex Group, the brand Pull&Bear was launched in 1991 with the intention of dressing young people. The brand has a network of 792 stores in 67 markets around the world (60 with physical stores and 7 online stores) and is planning to open 50 new stores in 2012/2013. In total 7,833 people work for Pull&Bear at the time this study was held. Pull&Bear has two different lines for men and women. One line is more casual in the form of sweatshirts, t-shirts, jeans, Bermuda shorts, plimsolls and hats, where cotton is the main fabric. The other line is more focused on adult male and female consumers who have grown up with the brand and want to dress up for work. Pull&Bear engages online with customers, beside their own blog page, by using Facebook, Twitter, Youtube, Vimeo and Pinterest. Additionally customers have the opportunity to sign up for an online newsletter or join an online photo booth to view pictures which were taken at the stores (Pullandbear, 2012).

4.6 Conclusion

The social media performance of all the above mentioned brands were observed online on a daily basis within one month. Brands like Massimo Dutti, Zara and Pull&Bear are owned by Inditex. Hence differences and similarities in the use of their social media can be observed to figure out if they all use an overall social media strategy or if each brand has their own strategic approach. The following Table 4 summarises the different brand details given in this chapter.

Table 3   Key Facts Fashion Brands

Brand	Country of Origin	Foundation Year	Genre	Social Media
Burberry	United Kingdom	1856	Luxury	Facebook, Twitter, Youtube, Instagram, Pinterest
COS	Sweden	2007	Moderate	Facebook, Youtube
Gucci	Italy	1921	Luxury	Facebook, Twitter, Youtube
H&M	Sweden	1979	Mass	Facebook, Twitter, Youtube, Instagram, Google+
Hollister	USA	2000	Moderate	Facebook, Twitter
Hugo Boss	Germany	1924	Luxury	Facebook, Twitter, Youtube, Google+, Foresquare, Instagram, Pinterest
Massimo Dutti	Spain	1985	Moderate	Facebook, Twitter, Youtube, Pinterest, Tublr
Louis Vuitton	France	1987	Luxury	Facebook, Twitter, Youtube
Pull&Bear	Spain	1991	Mass	Facebook, Twitter, Youtube, Pinterest , Vimeo
Reiss	United Kingdom	1971	Moderate	Facebook, Twitter, Youtube, Pinterest, Tumblr, Google+
Topshop	United Kingdom	1964	Mass	Facebook, Twitter, Youtube, Pinterest, Tumblr, Instagram, Google+
Zara	Spain	1975	Mass	Facebook, Youtube

5. Research Findings and Discussion

5.1 Introduction

This chapter presents the findings of the online observations, online user questionnaire and interviews with marketers. A discussion section is included in this chapter. This section critically analyses and interprets the methodology, research findings, and the relationship between the findings and other research. Weaknesses and limitations will be shown and approaches to overcome these. At the end of the discussion section a strategic plan for the successful use of social media is provided. Major highlights of this chapter are the developed strategic plan, a developed social media performance matrix and a social media mix chart.

5.2 Online Observations

As mentioned in the Methodology chapter of this study the implemented online observations concerning the social media activity of the twelve fashion labels are based on the three main social media applications Facebook, Twitter and Youtube. The findings about the brands' performances at each of these platforms will be discussed separately.

5.2.1 Facebook

The social networking page Facebook was at the time of this study the most popular social media application on the web (Henshell, 2012). In October 2012 one billion active users per month were measured, where 81% of these were from outside the USA and Canada. Facebook was created in 2004 to connect people and enable them to express and share what matters to them (Facebook, 2012b). Over the years the application has integrated a variety of tools for business marketing purposes. Brands now have their own Facebook pages to interact with customers and inform them of business news.

The findings of the online observations concerning the brands' interaction on Facebook include the number of fans a brand had at the beginning of the observation and at the end. Furthermore the number of posts a brand did per month and the amount of user engagement, which consists of the number of likes, comments and shares made by users. Therefore observations have shown that the number of a brand's fans on Facebook vary from one brand to another. At the end of the observation process the brand with the highest amount of fans was Zara with 14,103,638[1] users who liked the brand. In contrast the medium priced brand COS had the lowest amount of fans with 28,008 likes. Figure 5.1 shows the number of fans of all the twelve observed brands sorted from the platform with the highest amount to the one with the lowest. The green segments symbolize the growth rate within the one month observation period. The three fastest growing brand pages on Facebook were Louis Vuitton (+651,192), Hugo Boss (+384,760) and Hollister (+345,603). Whereas, pages like Zara (14,103,638), Burberry (13,205,100) and H&M (11,718,174) were the most popular pages with the highest amount of fans.

Figure 5.1 Fan Growth Rate Facebook

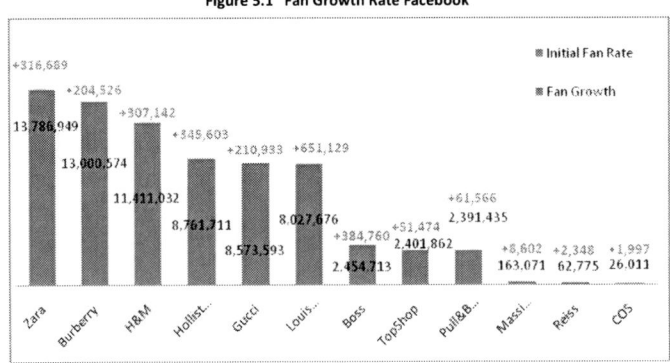

All of the twelve observed brands created and shared content in the form of wall posts on their page. All fashion brands had 'open' accessible pages, which means a user does not have to like a brand first and become a fan to view the shared content. Most of the brands created content on a daily basis. Between one and three posts were made per day; except on the weekends where only a few brands created posts. As the calculation in Figure 5.2 of the arithmetic mean of made wall posts below shows, one brand created on average 32 wall posts per month.

---

[1] Numbers are in thousand and represent the final amount of fans at the end of the observation process.

Therefore all posts made by the brands per month were added up and divided by 12, which is the number of observed brands. However, Zara and COS created content rather irregularly during the entire observation process and were the two brands with the lowest amount of created wall posts. Figure 5.3 shows that Zara made four posts within one month. In contrast Topshop was one of the most active brands on Facebook with 94 wall posts in total. Eight Facebook posts during one day was the highest amount they made and on average the brand created three wall posts per day (Table A10.1, Appendix). Reiss in comparison to Topshop was more moderate in creating wall posts with one post daily on average.

Apparent from the findings, almost each single post included at least one picture or video. As it can be seen in Figure 5.3 out of Topshop's 94 made wall posts, 90 included a video or picture. The most common type of multimedia posts included advertising pictures or campaign photos, which show the latest products of the brands. Some brands, like Hugo Boss or Topshop, regularly included links in their posts which took the users to the brand's other social media platforms, online shops or to their main website. A good linking strategy enables the companies to navigate traffic in the form of mouse clicks from one social media platform to another and takes the user on a journey through the brands images and products. In general the posts were mainly about new products, product promotions, seasonal sales, store openings, latest fashion trends, fashion shows and news about the fashion industry. Only the luxury brand Burberry, during the observation period, started creating daily posts about the weather in London. It is questionable if this is a successful strategy to increase brand awareness and to engage with the users as the shared content does not either relate to the brand nor to the fashion industry. However after the observation period these kinds of daily posts stopped and Burberry's social media manager left the company to join the Nike Group (Shearman, 2012).

Figure 5.2 Average Post Rate Facebook

$$\bar{x}_{\text{arithm}} = \frac{1}{n} \sum_{i=1}^{n} x_i = \frac{x_1 + x_2 + \cdots + x_n}{n}$$

$$= \frac{(94 + 43 + 42 + 36 + 30 + 29 + 27 + 23 + 23 + 17 + 11 + 4)}{12} = 31.5833$$

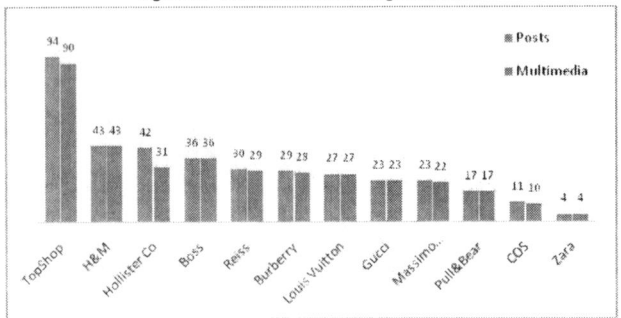
Figure 5.3 Facebook Posts including Multimedia

Furthermore out of the collected data from likes, comments and shares which users made to the brands' wall posts, the researcher was able to calculate the rate of user engagement. Figure 5.4 illustrates the user engagement on Facebook with the twelve fashion brands. The value in percentage includes all the likes, comments and shares made by the users for a brand's posts during one month. As it can be seen the three luxury brands Luis Vuitton (27%), Burberry (20.3%) and Gucci (17.4%) have the highest amount of user engagement. Luis Vuitton got in total during one month 427,921 likes, 8,322 comments and 20,800 shares to their created wall posts. For Zara and the medium priced labels Reiss and COS, only a small rate of user engagement could be measured. In comparison to the other brands their user engagement rate is less than 0.5%. The engagement of the brands with its fans, is determined by answering user questions or in general replying to user comments. Findings show, that only five of twelve brands engaged with their audience, two on a regular basis. This is illustrated in Figure 5.5. However it is worth noting that Massimo Dutti engaged with users only by liking all the comments that were made. This shows, at least to the user, that the comments were noticed by the marketers which makes a brand more approachable. H&M is the best example of how a company should engage with their customers via Facebook. The brand replied to all concerns users have, no matter if it is about product enquiries or purchase complaints. Hence H&M uses Facebook as a customer service and marketing tool.

Figure 5.4   User Engagement Facebook

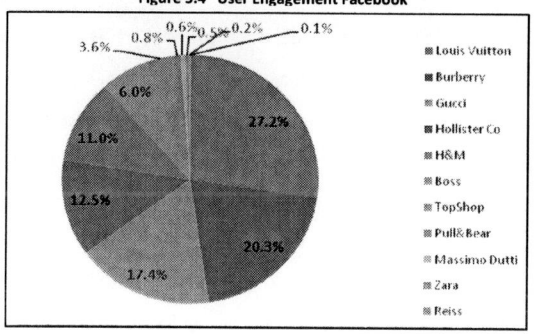

Figure 5.5   Facebook Brand Replies

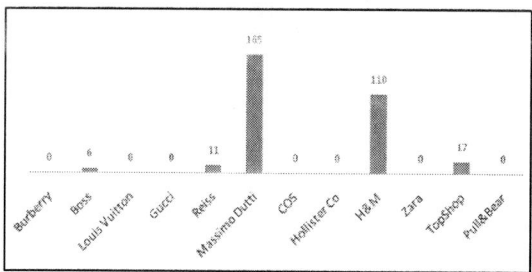

5.2.2   Twitter

Twitter is a real-time information network that allows brands to quickly share information about products or services with consumers and gather market intelligence along with feedback on the basis of small bursts of information called "tweets" (Twitter, 2012a). At the time of this study, Twitter had more than 140 Million active users from all over the world. Daily up to 340 Million tweets were created by users and businesses (stated: October 2012). For businesses and brands the conversations on Twitter provide a profitable basis about users' interests as well as what they want to engage with. The shared information can be used by businesses to participate in the online conversations and to drive consumer action with integrated campaigns (Twitter, 2012b).

46

The findings of the online observations concerning the brands' interaction on Twitter include the number of followers a brand had at the beginning of the observation and at the end, the number of tweets made by a brand per month and the amount of user engagement, measured by the number of user retweets and user replies. Findings show that the number of a brand's followers on Twitter vary from one brand to another. This is similar to the observations on Facebook. The brand with the highest amount of followers and fastest growing on Twitter was H&M with 1,393,006 followers (stated: August 2012). More than 106 thousand users started following the brand during the observation period. Brands like COS and Zara did not have a Twitter account. Figure 5.6 shows the number of followers of all the twelve observed brands sorted from the platform with the highest amount to the one with the lowest, including the growth rate.

Figure 5.6   Follower Growth Rate Twitter

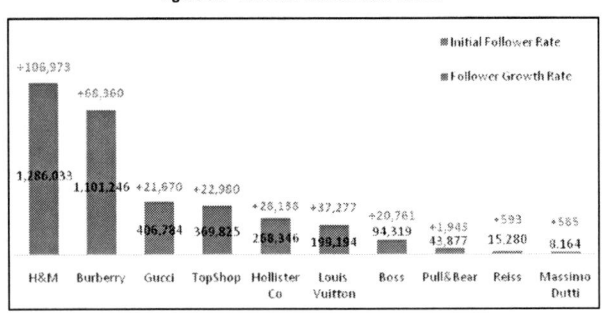

According to the amount of shared tweets during the research process, eight out of ten brands tweeted on a daily basis. The luxury brand Gucci and the medium priced brand Massimo Dutti tweeted rather infrequently. On average 79 tweets were created by one brand per month, which is a daily post rate between two and three tweets (Table A10.2). As well as for Facebook, Topshop was the most active brand at Twitter and made up to 332 tweets within one month. The brand tweeted several times a day. The tweets were about new products, store openings, current promotions and designer co-operations but also about the fashion industry and fashion trends in general. The tweets were complemented by links to encourage followers to also access Topshops's blog, its online magazine and its Facebook and Google+ pages. Thereby Topshop integrated Twitter into their overall digital strategy and built an alignment between the different online communication channels (Achenbach, 2012b). Figure 5.7 shows the number of posts created by the brands on Twitter during the observation period.

Figure 5.7 Twitter Posts

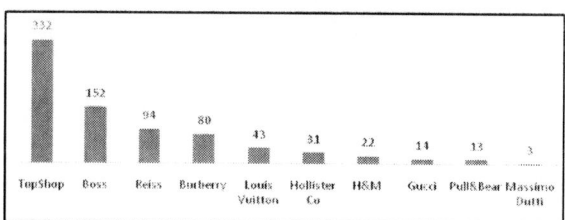

The general users engagement on Twitter was measured as well. This is determined by retweets and replies users made to a brand's tweets. Retweeting a tweet is comparable to sharing a post on Facebook. The brand's tweet will appear on the profile of the retweeter and is visible for their followers. On Twitter the three main fashion brands users liked to engage with were Burberry (37,4%), Topshop (23%) and H&M (16,8%). On a single day Burberry created three tweets which were shared by 568 users. It must be noted that the tweets can be viewed and shared by followers as well as by non-followers. Hence no conclusions can be made if the 568 users were all followers of the brand or if the number includes non-followers as well. Furthermore it is noticeable that the medium priced brand Reiss only gained users attention and retweets on Twitter through fashion related content. All tweets which did not concern a fashion topic got neither commented on, nor shared by users. This indicates a low engagement rate of less than 1%; illustrated in Figure 5.8. H&M used Twitter as well as Facebook as a customer service tool. Questions about online purchases, products or store opening times and any other customer concerns were directly responded to by H&M.

Figure 5.8   User Engagement Twitter

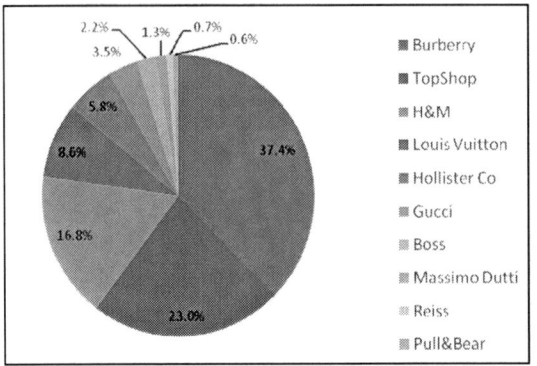

5.2.3   Youtube

The video sharing platform Youtube was, beside Facebook and Twitter, the most popular social media application at the time of this study (marketingprofs.com, 2011). It is available in 60 different languages across 43 countries in the world. Over 800 million users visit Youtube every month; with more than 100 million people taking a social action each week (liking, sharing, commenting) on the platform (Stated: October 2012). It enables users and businesses to discover, watch and share created videos (Youtube, 2012). In particular fashion brands can create their own account on Youtube to publish their new seasonal fashion campaigns or other fashion related videos. Users are able to subscribe to a brand's profiles on Youtube to keep up on their activity on the site (Youtube, 2012).

Observational findings according to the twelve fashion brands have shown that all brands except Hollister used Youtube to promote their latest fashion campaigns or runway shows from international fashion weeks. A Youtube presence of Hollister was not detectable. The brands with the highest number of subscribers were Burberry (39,064) and H&M (20,343). Louis Vuitton was, as it was on Facebook, the fastest growing brand with 2,523 new subscribers on Youtube during the one month observation period (Stated: August 2012). Figure 5.9 shows the amount of a brands' subscribers on Youtube at the beginning of the observation period and their growth rates. However, in terms of word of mouth marketing and to promote

49

products, the numbers of people that viewed videos and shared them with other users are more important. To view a video on Youtube the user does not have to subscribe necessarily to a specific brand. Therefore the number of views can vary from the number of subscribers. In total Louis Vuitton was the brand with the most shared videos (27) as well as the most viewed ones, with almost 500 thousand views. In comparison Burberry created only seven videos during the observation period and got 12% less views than its competitor Louis Vuitton (see Figure 5.10).

In terms of user engagement, Burberry was the brand users engaged the most with by liking, disliking or commenting on videos. The amount of the users engagement rate is illustrate in Figure 5.11. Brands which performed rather sparely on Youtube are Gucci, Pull&Bear and Reiss. In particular Reiss had a Youtube presence but did not share any new videos on its profile during the observation period. The luxury brand Gucci shared one single campaign video but had in total one of the most viewed Youtube profiles (Figure A11, Appendix). Generally the luxury fashion brands were more active in total on Youtube than at the other platforms and their videos attracted in sum the overall attention of users.

Figure 5.9 Subscriber Growth Rate Youtube

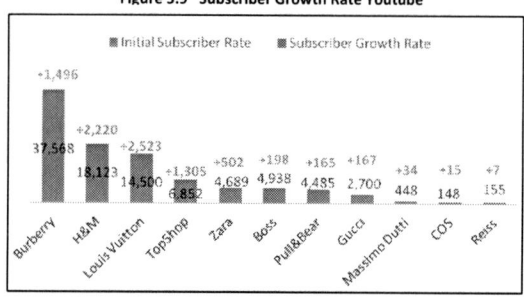

Figure 5.10 Youtube Posts

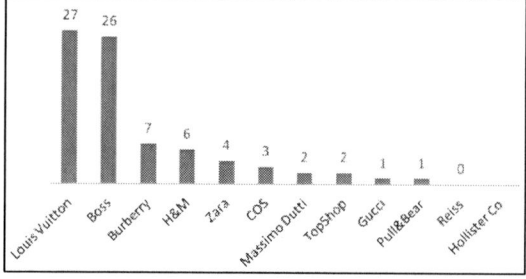

Figure 5.11   User Engagement Youtube

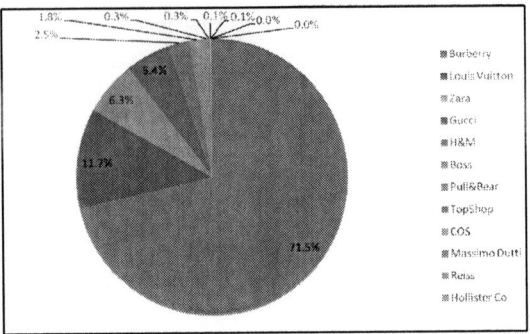

5.3 User Questionnaire

An online questionnaire was created to support and allow a comparison with the findings of the online observations as well as already existing theories. 50 social media users were contacted on Facebook and Twitter to answer ten questions related to their behavior and activity on social networking platforms. In relation to the users' demography, previous studies have shown that the average user of social networking pages are women between 18 and 34 years with a household income of less than $50,000 per year (Nielsen, 2011). The complete questionnaire used, including the results, can be viewed in the Appendix of this study (Appendix B).

The results of the online questionnaire have shown that the main social media platforms users were registered with, were Facebook, Twitter, Youtube and Google+. Every respondent had at least an account on Facebook and used it regularly. Whereas around 50% of the users were additionally registered with Twitter, Youtube and/or Google+. Fashion blogs were not as popular and barely viewed. The platforms with the most user activities, which includes reading and posting, was therefore Facebook. More than 90% see themselves as a high to moderate user on Facebook during the day. Youtube was the platform with the second largest amount of daily user activity. Up to 50% used the video sharing platform frequently. The majority (60%) used social media applications predominantly in the evening. The participants main activities on these platforms

51

were based on liking and commenting on posts from other users or brands along with sharing pictures. Only 5% used social media applications for criticism or making complaints. According to chapter 2 and the discussed study of Fournier and Avery (2011), concerning the power of users on social media platform, the participants of this survey did not feel that they can influence marketers or in particular the fashion industry by using social media. However, they believed that they can influence other users' opinions by using social media. Furthermore 36% of the users were following a brand to receive information about product promotions, sales and store openings. Whereas an additional 35% felt, that following a brand on social media is an easy and fast way to keep up to date with latest trends for their own benefit as well as for the brand itself. 24% followed a brand because they admired it.

Finally further results have shown that the most users follow brands like H&M, Zara and Topshop. This supports the findings of the online observations, where H&M (62%) and Zara (60%) are two of the main three brands with the most followers. It is evident that most people included within the questionnaire are following the lower priced brands. This can be attributable to the demography of the main social media users, aged between 18 and 34, with a household income of less than §50,000 per year (Nielsen, 2011). Due to the user demography and the content that the brands created on social media platforms, this user group (between 18 and 34) can be more easily related to the brands H&M and Zara.

5.4 Interviews

The final stage of the research process included interviews with marketers from the fashion industry. The main purpose was to identify the awareness marketers have of working with social media. Furthermore this allowed a comparison to be made between the users and marketers behavior on social media platforms. The five interviewed professionals were all related to the fashion industry and worked with social media before. The complete questionnaire is attached in the Appendix of this study (Appendix C).

One of the interviewees worked as a Business Development Manager for a small lifestyle and luggage company and was responsible for the social media presence of the company's products at the time of the study. For the last two years the company actively engaged on Facebook, Twitter, Pinterest, Instegram and Google+. With Facebook and Twitter being daily updated, Pinterest and Instegram were updated two to three times a week. Google+ less frequently,every two weeks.

Overall all of the interviewees were using the three main social media platforms (Facebook, Twitter, Youtube) for their businesses. Some included Google+ and some the picture sharing application Pinterest. The main purpose for using social media is to create brand engagement and brand awareness. Furthermore they used social media to inform users about their products, offers and special promotions. Some included social media into their communication strategy to provide customer services. The majority of marketers included photos and videos to engage with the users. This validates the findings of the observational research and is seen as more efficient by the marketers to get a user's attention. The mornings and evenings are stated as the best times to reach the most people by posts. However, as already mentioned in chapter 2, there are issues marketers have to deal with concerning critique and negative comments. The interviewees experienced a lot of negativity on social media platforms. The study by Matthew Lee (2006) and Fournier and Avery (2011), showed that the most common reason for users to join a community is their responsibility to tell others about their experiences. Those can be positive but also negative. Furthermore, as the results of the user questionnaires have shown, the majority of the social media users believed their social media performance had an impact on the opinion formation of other users. Nevertheless, the marketers seem to be aware of that issue and the power users can have to influence others in their opinion. Hence all of the interviewees for this study tried to engage with the users by directly replying to negative statements and be always being polite and honest. One of the interviewees stated, that many negative commenters have turned into happy customers after their problems were solved publicly via a social media platform such as Twitter. Another issue that concerned the marketers is the measurement of their social media activity. They have admitted that there is currently no standardised method to measure the Return on Investment (ROI). Some were counting the followers of their pages, some were using analytic tools like Google Analytics to see how much traffic (in the form of clicks) went through their social media pages to their website. However, these methods are not sufficient enough to give significant statements of the successful use of social media. A standardised method would be appreciated by all of the interviewees.

It seems, against the study by Fournier and Avery (2011), that marketers are aware of the importance of social media for their businesses. One interviewee stated, due to the fast paced and highly visual nature of the fashion industry, social media makes it easy to attract new customers and engage with them in a more personal way, in comparison to other marketing tools and PR methods. "It is an ideal chance for brands to have a voice through these channels and build a strong community. It is also a very cost effective way of marketing." But they warn of an overload of shared content and of having too many platforms at one time. The majority rather focused on certain platforms instead of being present at every existing platform. Furthermore, as there is never full control over the shared content, marketers need to pay consistent attention to their social media platforms. Therefore, a large investment of time and effort is required.

5.5 Discussion

This section includes a critical analysis and interpretation of the research findings in relation to the research question and objectives set out for this study. The relationship between the findings and other research is clearly stated. Furthermore weaknesses and limitations of the research process are also mentioned in this section. At the end a social media strategic plan for businesses will be presented, which was developed by the researcher in relation to his findings. This helps businesses to overcome weaknesses of social media and can be used as an overall guideline to include social media in a company's business strategy more successfully. The main purpose of this study was to define the importance of social media for the fashion industry. This was based on the aim and the nine objectives listed in chapter 1. Hence the viewed secondary literature, the findings of the online observations, the conducted online questionnaire and the interviews with marketers enabled the researcher to formulate an accurate conclusion about the importance of social media for the fashion industry. Due to the fast changing environment of the internet and technology, conclusions in this section are based on the recent secondary literature and the data collected during this study.

Overall, findings have shown, that the use and the engagement of brands with social media differ widely within the fashion industry. Referring to the used methodology for the observation process, the researcher is able to compare the brands' performances on social media platforms and to make assumptions about the generic social media behaviour of fashion brands. Therefore the tested social media measurement methods, from secondary literature, were proved partly as efficient and partly as not useful. The method Hoffman and Fodor (2010) used in their paper "Can You Measure the ROI of Your Social Media Marketing?" was the most efficient one and helped the researcher to accomplish the online observations. Hence, focusing on the users' key motivation factors (Connection, Creation, Consumption, Control) makes social media activity measureable and comparable. By counting users' likes, comments and shares then comparing them to the number of a brand's posts, statements can be made about the users' engagement rate with the brand.

A less efficient method for measuring social media activity is based on the formulas to calculate the engagement rate. Both types of formulas, the one from Socialbakers (2012c) as well as the one from Wisemetrics (2012), were tested and then proved by the researcher as insignificant. The calculated values are not comparable to each other. Therefore, the researcher can support Wisemetrics' critique about the formula from Socialbakers (2012c). Additionally, the researcher found out that, the higher the amount of a brand's followers, the lower the resulting engagement rate. This is controversial, as the engagement rate should be higher when more users are interested in the brand and follow them. Furthermore the formula developed by Wisemetrics (2012) addresses the actual amount of reached users. Reached users include users that are not necessarily following a brand but liking, commenting and sharing the brand's posts as well. But the measurement of the actual reached users was only on the video sharing platform Youtube possible, by the number of video views. This led to the same insignificant results as the previous formula from Socialbakers (2012c). The findings are listed in the Appendix (Table A4.1; A4.2). The researcher decided not to include these formulas in his analysis process.

To overcome the weaknesses in measurement and to make the findings of the online observations comparable, the researcher developed the measurement tool of Hoffman and Fodor (2010) further. A Social Media Performance Matrix (SMP-Matrix) (see Figure 5.12) was developed based on the already existing Boston Consulting Matrix (BCG-Matrix) (Schermerhorn, 2010, p. 149, fig. 7.5). The matrix helps to determine a brand's social media performance in comparison to their competitors' brands or alternatively a company's other brands. The SMP-Matrix evaluates comparative advantage indicated by social media leadership. It consists of four cells (Freshman, Shining Star, Sloth, Shy Bird), where the horizontal axis denotes the brand's social media activity and the vertical axis represents the users' social media engagement. Furthermore each of the four cells represent a particular type of social media brand performance. The four different types of cells are illustrated in Figure 5.12 and defined as follows by the researcher:

Figure 5.12 Social Media Performance Matrix

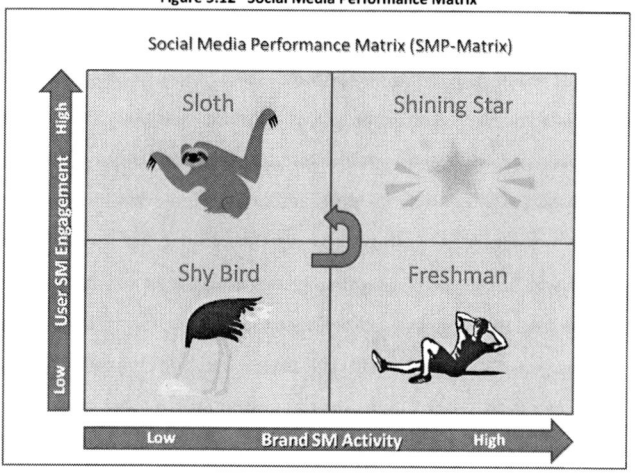

56

Shy Bird - Brands placed in this cell have a low user engagement as well as a low activity on social media platforms. These brands mainly rely on traditional offline marketing tools and are not aware of how to use social media for their purposes effectively. The brands shy away from communicating with users. Posts are rarely shared, with a maximum of three posts per week. A linking strategy does not exist. They are not publishing their social media presences on their websites. Hence users can not engage with the brand as there is nothing to engage with and therefore they shy away as well. These brands do not know how to implement social media in their business strategy efficiently and need to improve at first their shared content. By posting out more regularly, every day or every second day, brand related content including promotions should attract the users attention. The brand has to start improving their social media activity to raise the users social media engagement.

Freshman - Freshman represents brands with a high activity on social media platforms. They are creating different kinds of posts several times a day and using a variety of social media applications. The brands placed in this cell have mostly a small but growing number of followers. Nevertheless, these brands address only a small number of users and need to improve their linking strategy and their shared content. The content needs to be more user engaging and related to the brand image. Online promotions and free giveaways shared on the social media platforms are a good way to improve the users' engagement.

Shining Star - Shining Star includes brands that perform well on social media platforms and are aware of the importance that social media can have. They integrated social media as a strategy tool in their business plan. The brands have a high social media activity and a high number of users that daily post, like, comment and share the created content on different social media platforms. The created content fits to the brand's image and engages the users. The several social media platforms are well linked with each other as well as to the main website. The shared posts include links to the brand's other social media platforms. Users can benefit daily from the brand's created posts. The brand uses social media effectively as a marketing, customer service, advertising and research tool altogether. Their number of followers is rapidly growing. The brand need to focus on new trends concerning social media and keep up to date with new technological innovations. In addition, competitors' social media behaviour should be analysed to address weaknesses or strengths for a competitive advantage.

Sloth - A sloth is loved by everyone, in the zoo many visitors like watching it, but it does not do much during the day to engage with its visitors. Similarly the brands placed in this cell are inactive. A high number of user follow a brand and like to engage with the shared content, but the brand does not use social media on a regular basis. Posts are created every third day or less. The posts are more informative than engaging and mainly based on advertising posts. It seems to be an acceptable position for a brand, but not effective in the case of increasing online and offline purchases by informing users about products. Furthermore it is dangerous, as users can get bored and thus not see a reason in following anymore. Users might lose interest in the brand which can affect their future buying behaviour. The brand should try to vary their content and publish it on a regular basis to keep users engaged. They have a high potential to reach a high number of users. Users are willing to engage with the brand.

Most brands might start off as a Shy Bird but as soon as they increase their social media activity, they become Freshman. Depending on the type of shared content and successful social media integration, more users might start to engage with the brand. This brings the brand to a Shining Star position. Should the brand start being less active than before, it might risk to lose their Shining Star position and become a Sloth. The Sloth position is dangerous as users might lose interest in the brand and stop following it, which brings the brand back to the Shy Bird position.

To apply the above SMP-Matrix to the twelve observed fashion brands the researcher counted the posts from all three social media platforms together and created a total for each brand. Afterwards a ranking was formed from 1 being the least active brand, to 12 the most active brand. This represents the independent variable and horizontal scale; the brands' social media activity. The vertical scale (dependent variable) represents the user's engagement with the brands. The users' likes, shares and comments from all three social media platforms were counted together and ranked from 1 being the brand users engage least with, to 12 the brand users engage most with. Figure 5.13 shows the SMP-Matrix including the results of the twelve fashion brands' social media performances during an observation period of one month, July 2012. The size of the circles represents the amount of a brand's followers. The measurement is based on the total of all included platforms. If required the matrix can also be used to illustrate the performances for only one specific social media platform or for one company's portfolio. Depending on the kind of industry a recalibration of the scaling might be necessary.

Figure 5.13   Brands' Social Media Performances

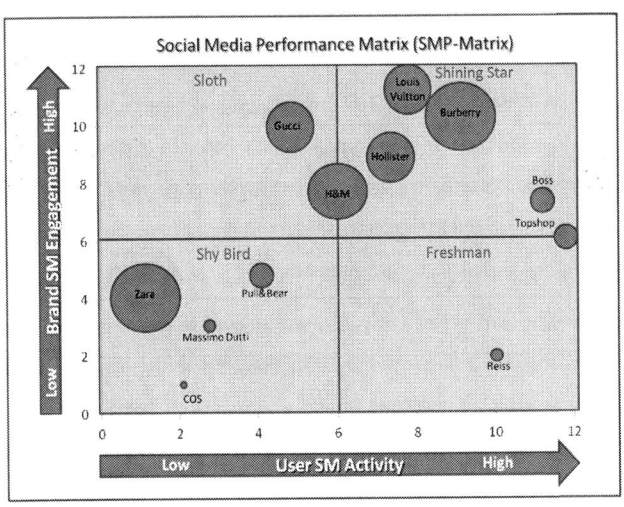

The above SMP-Matrix (Figure 5.13) shows, some brands engaged on a regular basis with their followers and already included social media in their marketing strategy. Whereas others have a social media presence but do not use it effectively to strengthen their brand awareness and take advantage of it. For example the luxury fashion brand Gucci had, in comparison to the other observed fashion brands, a considerable amount of followers which were willing to engage with the brand. The brand showed a reserved performance and preferred rather not to engage with the users. Enquiries or comments of users were all ignored by the brand's marketers. In general, conclusions can be made that luxury fashion brands reply infrequently and rather less to user enquiries on social media platforms. Nevertheless these brands attract a lot of attention on social media platforms and users are motivated to engage with the brands. As can be seen in Figure 5.13. Overall, three of four luxury brands are placed in the Shining Star cell, which indicates an high awareness of social media as a strategic tool. The brands had a high social media activity during the observation period and a high number of users that on a daily basis like, comment and share the created content. The several social media platform were well linked with each other and to the main website. The shared posts included links to the brand's other social media platforms and fitted with the brands image to engage the users.

Only Burberry attracted negative attention. The brand created and shared a video campaign in accordance with the American Independence Day on Youtube, Twitter and Facebook. The campaign included the brand's name, a firework in the national colours red, white and blue and the slogan "Happy 4th July". It is well known that each year on the 4th of July the Americans celebrate their independence from the British Empire. Burberry, as a traditional British clothing brand, attracted a lot of negative attention as users found the video campaign rather ironic and less meaningful (Burberry, 2012b). However, Louis Vuitton, Burberry and Gucci (all luxury brands) are in total the top three brands users engage with. Even if they do not create content on a regular basis as the low priced brands like Topshop and H&M do. Medium priced brands like Reiss, Massimo Dutti or COS seem to struggle with social media. Their user engagement is overall low and posts are mostly not related to fashion content which appears to keep the number of followers small. Reasons can be referred back to the company's non awareness of the importance of social media.

The best example is Inditex which owns the brands Massimo Dutti, Zara and Pull&Bear. All brands of the company had in total a low social media performance and need to improve their online presence by creating more fashion related posts, sharing content users can benefit from and linking all social media platforms together. Hence it can be stated that the performance on social media platforms depends on the company's awareness of social media for their business. Zara has, due to its number of followers (14,108,829), a high potential to become a Shining Star. But during the observation period the brand did not use social media frequently and actively enough to grow their engagement with their users. Only Reiss seems to be aware of social media potential and used it regularly. The content needs to be more user engaging and related to the brand's image. Online promotions and free giveaways, shared on the social media platforms, are a good way to improve the users' engagement.

According to the brands' number of followers, the researcher has discovered that many other companies (not included in this study) buy followers to increase their number and hence get a higher ranking in search engines like Google. This higher ranking brings the companies more online clicks and visits on their website or social media platforms (cf. Barone, 2011). Therefore, these numbers need to be considered carefully, as there are clear doubts about their credibility.

Strategic Plan

The findings of this study have shown that the marketers are aware of the importance of social media for their business. This matches the results of the 2012 Social Media Marketing Industry Report, where out of 3,800 marketers from different industries, 83% of the interviewees indicated that social media is an important tool for their business growth. Companies that included social media in their marketing strategy reported an increase in their market exposure and in their sales (Stelzner, 2012). However, the majority of surveyed companies have no clear objectives for their social media strategies (Econsultancy, 2012). An overall guideline for a successful social media integration and management is demanded by marketers and is necessary for the future growth of their businesses. Therefore the researcher of this study developed a strategic plan. The plan can be used by businesses as a guide to successfully integrate social media in their marketing strategy. It includes the following three steps:

In the first step of the plan, the business needs to set clear goals and define their objectives for the use of social media. What will be achieved by implementing social media in the marketing strategy is the emerging question here. The set social media objectives should be aligned to the company's own business goals. The majority of the interviewed companies are using social media mainly for enhancing their customer service, increasing their brand awareness and informing users about product promotions. Furthermore key users can be identified with the help of social media. Additionally a brand's performance can be analysed in comparison to their competitors' performances.

Figure 5.14 illustrates four business functions (Marketing, Customer Service, Advertising and Market Research) that social media should address as a strategic tool. It is advisable to include all four functions in the social media strategy to successfully address the target user and gain the most benefit from social media. The low priced fashion brand H&M is a good example of a successful social media adopter. The brand answered customer enquiries and concerns daily on Facebook and Twitter (Customer Service), used product promotions to attract the users attention (Marketing), placed new product campaigns to inform the user (Advertising) and used user comments to improve their service (Market Research).

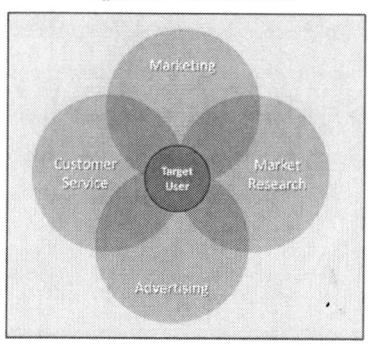

Figure 5.14 Social Media Mix

Subsequently, the right type of social media application need to be chosen carefully. As findings have shown it is not essential to have a social media presence on each existing platform. The focus should lie on three main social media platforms. The suitable form of the application depends on the business' target group to be reached and the type of messages to be created (Kaplan and Haenlein, 2010). The picture sharing platform Pinterest, for example, is more applicable for the fashion industry rather than for the book industry, where a content orientated platform like Wordpress.com would be more suitable. Users of this can create their own blogs and share self written novels. Furthermore it is helpful to consider previous statistics about the most popular social media platforms for the decision making process. Based on the findings Facebook is currently the most used platform for both users and companies. As such a company should have at least a Facebook profile to engage with consumers.

The second stage of the social media strategic plan includes a predetermination of the content that will be shared on social media platforms. The number of daily created messages, the time of the day, the kinds of posts and the included media need to be considered. According to the interviews with marketers, conclusions can be made that three messages per day are sufficient to improve brand awareness. Creating posts every second day on one specific platform is also sufficient. Different platforms can also be used alternately. This ensures that the user has something new to discover on various platforms each day. However, it is important not to overload the user with content nor to use social media as a direct sales tool. Users want to engage with a brand on social media platforms, because they like the image the brand creates and not to purchase goods (Laurent, 2012). Furthermore the shared content should benefit the user and should support the general communicated brand image. Only when users can get benefits out of the posts they will like and share those with other users. By offering promotions or free giveaways, users will start following quickly and brand awareness will increase (Junghenn, 2012).

Concerning Burberry's created video campaign for the 4th July in the USA, the luxury brand had to learn the hard way what is means not to share brand related content. In addition, the brand created, over a period of two months, daily, three to five posts about the weather in London. Each post included a picture of the weather and was shared on Facebook and Twitter at the same time. Due to the interviews with marketers, it can be stated that the shared content should vary between the different platforms. One user might use Facebook and Twitter at the same time. Hence, to make it more interesting for users to discover the brand's activities, posts need to fit to the application. A Twitter post should be shorter and more concise in its form than a post on Facebook. As observations have shown, posts with at least one picture or video are seen by more users than posts without any media. Moreover the most effective times of posting during the day are the morning and evening. Besides creating wall posts, it is important for a company to stay engaged in conversations with users. A frequent review of the comments or enquiries users' made is advisable. They like to see that they are heard and that there is someone human behind the brand. Therefore a marketer should always try to respond as soon as possible in a polite, friendly and honest way. Never ignoring a critique as critiques are made to gain useful information from (Junghenn, 2012). The medium priced brand Massimo Dutti shows their commitment to the user by liking every single post but the brand never replied to a user comment during the observation process. Finally, to improve the user traffic between different platforms, a company has to ensure that all social media platforms are searchable, visible and accessible to the public. This includes a good linking strategy between the website and all used social media applications.

The last stage of the strategic plan includes an analytical approach to measure the company's social media activity. Using analytic programs such as Google Analytics will give the marketer an idea about the user traffic, including from which platforms the redirected users are coming from and how many users have visited the brand's pages. As presented in this study, likes, shares and comments can be counted and compared with the number of posts to get an impression about the user engagement. A comparison with the competitors' user engagement within the same industry sector is also advisable. The developed social media measurement matrix might be a useful tool to place a brand's social media activity in comparison to their competitors. Finally, the marketers can learn from the users' comments and critiques. Therefore, the comments should be analysed to gain knowledge about consumers preferences. Figure 5.15 illustrates the strategic plan and its three stages.

Figure 5.15   Strategic Plan

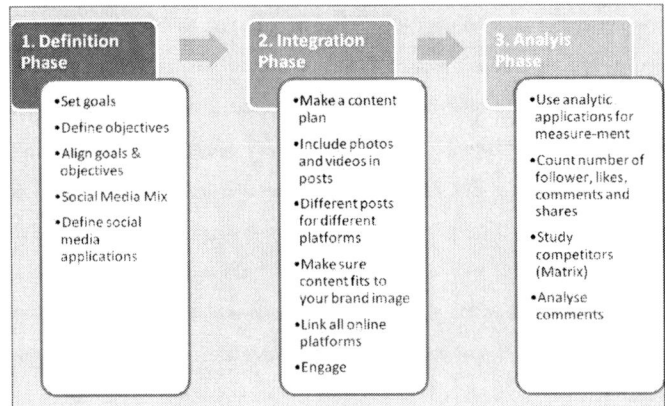

6. Conclusion and Recommendations

6.1 Conclusion

The main purpose of this research was to estimate the importance of social media for the fashion industry. This was driven by previous studies and published articles from Fournier and Avery (2011) and Socialbakers (2012) about the response rate of different industries on Facebook. These studies indicated that the fashion industry had low engagement with social media applications. Additionally, during the research process, weaknesses in the measurement of companies' social media activity appeared. Previous secondary literature has shown that companies struggle with analysing if their social media activities are successful and efficient. Hence, it became important to develop an efficient strategy for businesses to overcome these weaknesses.

For the investigation of this study's purpose and for the fulfilment of the associated objectives, an analytical research approach was developed, including an online observation of 12 international fashion labels, user questionnaires and interviews with marketers. Observation findings have shown that most brands used the video sharing platform YouTube to promote their latest fashion campaigns or runway shows from international fashion weeks. This new form of content sharing proved to be an efficient tool to reach the consumers and engage with them. However, in terms of word of mouth marketing and to promote products, it is important to know how many people viewed the content and shared it with others rather than how many users actually subscribed to the profile. Overall, findings have shown that the use, and hence the engagement of brands with social media differ widely within the fashion industry. Some brands engage on a regular basis with their followers and already include social media in their marketing strategy. Whereas other brands do not take advantage of social media to effectively strengthen their brand awareness.

Most social media users are registered with Facebook, Twitter, YouTube and Google+. Every respondent has an account on Facebook and uses it regularly. Most users are following low priced brands like H&M, Zara and Topshop. This can be referred back to the type of content brands created and the demography of the average social media user who is aged between 18 and 34, with a household income of less than $50,000 per year (Nielsen, 2011). Users want to receive a benefit in the form of product promotions, sales or free giveaways by following a brand on social media platforms. Furthermore they use social media to share their opinions about products or services with other users. It seems that marketers are aware of the influence users can have in the opinion creation process by using social media. The findings of this study show that marketers know the benefit social media can bring to building and strengthening a brand's image. Creating brand awareness, providing customer service and sharing product campaigns are the main reasons marketers use social media applications and this defines the importance of social media for the fashion industry. Furthermore, a social media mix helps marketers make the most of the different social media applications. Therefore social media is simultaneously used as a marketing, advertising, customer service and analytical tool. However, marketers still struggle in measuring their social media activities efficiently. A developed social media performance matrix helps to overcome these weaknesses in measurement. Furthermore, the SMP-Matrix will evaluate comparative strength indicated by social media leadership and allows companies to compare their social media activity with competitors.

Additionally, marketers can use a strategic plan to integrate social media successfully into their business. This ensures a precise integration of the different social media applications into a company's objectives and brand image. Overall, marketers still need to start engaging with users and frequently reply to user's enquiries. The content shared online contains useful information marketers can implement into their market research as well as in developing new products.

Finally, there is high potential in the fashion industry to use social media to effectively communicate new styles and trends. Due to the easy accessibility to photos and videos, social media enables fashion brands to have a fast and easy way of creating brand awareness and sharing advertising campaigns. Users like to keep up to date with the latest trends and products from their favourite brands on social media platforms. Style photos and campaign pictures are shared with other users.

Furthermore, social media offers the fashion industry a new way of conducting market research. The content users share contains information that can be used by brands to develop new trends and hence to gain a competitive advantage. However, there is still potential to improve the overall awareness of social media within the fashion industry in future. In the following section recommendations are made about the future research approach of this study.

6.2 Recommendations and Future Research

The study's findings have shown a high potential of engagement with customers by sharing photos and videos. Also the use of mobile devices such as smart phones or tablet PC's to enter social media platforms is becoming more important and increases the use of social media applications. Future research could be expanded on how companies engage with customers via mobile devices and what content is shared on those applications. An additional marketing strategy for a successful implementation of mobile applications would be necessary.

In relation to content creation and to overcome the limitations in the measurement of the immediate Return On Investment (ROI), businesses should focus on the content that is shared daily on their social media platforms. A content analysis includes an analytical approach to study the conversations people are having on social media platforms about a company's brand. In relation to this study, the twelve observed fashion brands could be monitored again to observe the shared content on the brands' social media platforms. The gathered qualitative information gives marketers indications of what customers require, what they like about the brand and its products and what they do not like. Marketing strategies can then be purposefully linked. This would replace the need for a statistical measurement method like the discussed ineffective formulas to calculate the engagement rate.

Furthermore, the brands' linking strategies will be included in future research. This contains an analysis of how these brands transfer user traffic in the form of clicks from page to page. To refer back to the results of this study, it is therefore important to have different ways to communicate and not to use the same syntax on each social media platform for example. A good linking strategy brings the brands more visitors and enables them to share more content on different platforms with a higher number of people. Also, the brands would be showing up more frequently in search engine results.

Finally, future research could include a larger number of observed brands. This supports the validity of the study's purpose and guarantees a more solid conclusion. In addition, brands from other industry sectors should be included and compared to the fashion industry. Findings from other sectors can also be used to support the use of social media for the fashion industry in future.

Steffen Achenbach
London South Bank University
December 2012

Bibliography

Achenbach, S. (2012a) *Potential Implications of Social Media*. Essay Marketing Communications, London: LSBU.

Achenbach, S. (2012b) *The Role of Social & Digital Media Technologies for the Fashion Company "Topman"*. Essay Social Media, London: LSBU.

Absatzwirtschaft (2009) *Nutzer betrachten Community-Engagement von Marken wohlwollend* [Online]. Available from: http://www.absatzwirtschaft.de/Content/ Communicat/news/b=67271, p=1003214, t=fthighlight,highlightkey=Social+Media [Accessed 25 March 2012].

Absatzwirtschaft (2010a) *Social Media-Werbung gewinnt weiter an Bedeutung.* [Online]. Available from: http://www.absatzwirtschaft.de/CONTENT/ Communication/news/ b=70632, p=1003214, t=fthighlight,highlightkey=Social+M ediaWerbung+gewinnt+Bedeutun. [Accessed 25 March 2012].

Absatzwirtschaft (2010b) *Social Media verlangt dialogischeres Vorgehen* [Online]. Available from: http://www.absatzwirtschaft.de/CONTENT/Communication/news b=69674, p=1003214 t=fthighlight,highlightkey=Social+Media+verlangt+dialogisch eres+Vorgehen. [Accessed 25 March 2012].

Advaithinfoserv.com (2012) *Face 2 Face.* [Online]. Available from: http://www.advaithinfoserv.com/f2f.html [Accessed 28 November 2012].

Baltner, U. (2010) *Vom Laufsteg ins Web 2.0: Die Social Media Aktivitäten der Mode Labels.* [Online]. Available from: http://www.slideshare.net/UweBaltner/ socialmediastrategien-der-modelabels-vom-laufsteg-ins-web-20 [Accessed 29 April 2012].

Barone, L. (2011) *Buying Facebook Fans is a Horrible Idea.*[Blog entry]. Available from: http://outspokenmedia.com/social-media/buying-facebook-fans/ [Accessed 29 October 2012].

BBC (2009) *Hollister branding 'fictitious.* [Online]. Available from: http://news.bbc.co.uk/1/hi/ business/8340453.stm [Accessed 28 November 2012].

Blackshaw, P. (2008) Shout Control: Who owns the influencer? *NewMedia Marketing Management AMA*, January 2008, pp. 52-54.

Boslaugh, S. (2007) Secondary Data Sources for Public Health. St. Louis: Hardback.

Braatz, K. (1988) Friedrich Nietzsche – Eine Studie zur Theorie der Öffentlichen Meinung, Band 18, Berlin: de Gruyter.

Bueno, B. J. (2007) Why we talk: the truth behind Word-of-Mouth—Seven reasons your customers will or will not talk about your brand, *Journal Of Advertising Research*, December, pp. 535-536.

Burberry (2012a) *About Burberry.* [Online]. Available from: http://www.burberryplc .com/about_burberry/our_strategy [Accessed 28 November 2012].

Burberry (2012b) *Happy 4th of July from Burberry* (2012) [Online video]. Available from: http://www.youtube.com/ watch?v=8Wj8h61c3Us [Accessed 25 October 2012].

Busemann, K. and Gscheidle, C. (2009) Web 2.0: Communitys bei jungen Nutzern beliebt, in: *Media Perspektiven*, 7 (7), pp. 356-364.

Businessdictionary.com (2012a) *Luxury Goods.* [Online]. Available from: http://www.businessdictionary.com/definition/luxury-goods.html [Accessed 28 November 2012].

Businessdictionary.com (2012b) *Brand Awareness.* [Online]. Available from: http://www.businessdictionary.com/definition/brand-awareness.html [Accessed 28 November 2012].

Cater-Steel, A. and Al-Hakim, L. (2009) Information Systems, Research Methods, Epistemology, And Applications. England: IGI Global.

Chaffey, D. et al. (2006) Internet Marketing: Strategy, Implementation and Practice, 3rd edn. England: Pearson Education Ltd.

Collinsdictionary.com (2012) *English Dictionary*. [Online]. Available from: http://www.collinsdictionary.com/dictionary/english/medium-priced [Accessed 28 November 2012].

Conceptofluxurybrands.com (2012) *The Definition of Luxury Brands*. [Online]. Available from: http://www.conceptofluxurybrands.com/concept/luxury-brands-definition [Accessed 28 November 2012].

Corey, L. G. (1971) People Who Claim to be Opinion Leaders: Identifying Their Characteristics by Self-report, *Journal of Marketing*, (35), pp. 48-53.

Cosstores (2012) *About Us*. [Online]. Available from: http://www.cosstores.com/ [Accessed 1 December 2012]

Datamonitor (2011) *Arcadia Group Limited*. [Online]. Available from: Datamonitor. http://www.google.co.uk/search?aq=f&ix=seb&sourceid=chrome&ie=UTF-8&q=eckige+klammer. [Accessed 28 March 2012].

Debono, J. (2012) *Social Media Etiquette-The Do's and Don'ts*. [Blog entry]. Available from: http://socialmediatoday.com/node/513583 [Accessed 24 November 2012].

De Vaus, D. A. (2001) Research design in social research. London: SAGE.

Dowling, G. and Weeks, W. (2011) Media analysis: what is it worth?, *Journal of Business Strategy*, 32 (1), pp. 26-33. [Online]. Available from: Emerald. http://emeraldinsight.com [Accessed 29 April 2012].

Döring, N. (2003) Sozialpsychologie des Internet: Die Bedeutung des Internet für Kommunikationsprozesse, Identitäten, soziale Beziehungen und Gruppen, 2. überarbeitete Auflage, Göttingen: Hogrefe.

Dressler, M. and Telle, G. (2009) *Meinungsführer in der interdisziplinären Forschung*, 1st edition, Wiesbaden: GWV Fachverlage.

Ebersbach, A., Glaser, M. and Heigl, R. (2008) *Social Web*. Konstanz: UVK Verlagsgesellschaft.

Eccleston, D. and Griseri, L. (2008) How does web 2.0 stretch traditional influencing patterns?, *International Journal of Market Research*, 50 (5), pp. 591-616.

Econsultancy (2012) *Quarterly Digital Intelligence Briefing: Managing and Measuring Social*. [Online]. Available from: http://econsultancy.com/us/reports /quarterly-digital-intelligence-briefing-managing-and-measuring-social [Assessed 20 September 2012].

Ehrlich, E.; Berg Flener, S.; Carruth, G.; Hawkins, J. (1980) *Oxford American Dictionary*. New York: Oxford University Press.

Facebook (2012a) *Facebook legal terms*. [Online]. Available from: http://www.facebook.com/ legal/terms [Accessed 14 Oktober 2012].

Facebook (2012b) *Key Facts*. [Online]. Available from: http://newsroom.fb.com/ content/default.aspx?NewsAreaId=22 [Accessed 28 Oktober 2012].

Fisch, M. and Gscheidle, C. (2008) Mitmachnetz Web 2.0: Rege Beteiligung nur in Communitys, Media Perspektiven, 7 (7), pp. 356-364.

Fisher, C. (2004) Researching and Writing a Dissertation for Business Students. Harlow: FT Prentice Hall – Pearson Education Limited.

Fournier, S. and Avery, J. (2011) The Uninvited Brand, *Business Horizons*, (54), pp. 193-207. [Online]. Available from: *Science Direct*. http://sciencedirect.com [Accessed 14 March 2012].

Friemel, T. N. (2010) Diffusionsforschung, in: Stegbauer, Christian; Häußling, Roger (Hrsg.): *Handbuch Netzwerkforschung*, Wiesbaden: VS Verlag für Sozialwissenschaften, pp. 825-833.

Ghauri, P. and Gronhaug, K. (2005) *Research Methods In Business Studies: A Practical Guide.* Essex: Prentice Hall Europe.

Gilbert, B. (2009) Ten surefire ways to fail in new media, *Admap Magazine,* [Online]. Available from: *WARC.* http://warc.com [Accessed 14 March 2012].

Gladwell, M. (2000) *The Tipping Point.* New York: Littel, Brown Company.

Goldenberg, J., Han, S., Lehmann, D. R. and Hong, J.W. (2009) The Role of Hubs in the Adoption Process, *Journal of Marketing,* 73 (2), pp. 1-13.

Götzenbrucker, G. (2005) *Soziale Netzwerke in Unternehmen: Potenziale computergestützter Kommunikation in Arbeitsprozessen.* Wiesbaden: Deutscher Universitäts-Verlag.

Graham, J., and Havlena, W. (2007) Finding the "Missing Link": Advertising's Impact on Word of Mouth,Web Searches, and Site Visits, *Journal of Advertising Research,* December, pp. 427-435.

Granovetter, M. S. (1973) The Strength of Weak Ties, *American Journal of Sociology,* 78 (6), pp. 1360-1380.

Hamann, G. (2008) Die Medien und das Medium: Web 2.0 verändert die Kommunikation der Gesellschaft, in: Meckel, M.; Stanoevska-Slabeva, K. (eds.): Web 2.0 – Die nächste Generation Internet, Baden-Baden: Nomos, S. 214-226.

Hennig-Thurau, T. and Gwinner K. P. (2004) Electronic Word-Of-Mouth Via Consumer-Opinion Platforms: What Motivates Consumers To Articulate On The Internet?, *Journal of Interactive Marketing* 18 (1), pp. 38-52.

Henshell, R. (2012) *Which Social Media Platform is Right For Your Business?.* [Blog entry]. Available from: http://socialmediatoday.com/james-debono/827961/which-social-media-platform-right-your-business [Accessed 24 November 2012].

H&M (2012) *About H&M.* [Online]. Available from: http://about.hm.com/content /hm/AboutSection/en/About.html [Accessed 28 November 2012].

Hooker, J. (2008) *Cultural Differences in Business Communication*. Research Paper Business Communication, Pittsburgh: Tepper School of Business. [Online]. Available from: http://ba.gsia.cmu. edu/jnh/businesscommunication.pdf [Accessed 7 May 2012].

Hoffman, D.L. and Fodor, M. (2010) Can You Measure The ROI Of Your Social Media Marketing?, *MIT Sloan Management Review*, 52 (1), pp. 41-49.

Hollenbeck, C. R. and Zinkhan, G. M. (2006) Consumer Activism on the Internet: The Role of Anti-brand Communities, *Advances in Consumer Research* , (33), pp. 479-485.

Högg, R., Martignoni, R., Meckel, M and Stanoevska-Slabeva, K. (2008). Web 2.0 Geschäftsmodelle, in: Meckel, M. and Stanoevska-Slabeva, K. (eds.) Web 2.0 – Die nächste Generation Internet. Baden-Baden: Nomos, pp. 39-58.

Huang, C., Shen,Y., Lin, H. and Chang, S. (2007) Bloggers' Motivations and Behaviors: A Model, *Journal of Advertising Research*, December, pp. 472-484.

Hugoboss (2012) *The Hugo Boss Group.* [Online]. Available from: http://group.hugoboss.com/en/corporate_profile.htm [Accessed 28 November 2012].

Inditex (2012) *Who we are: Timeline.* [Online]. Available from: http://www.inditex.com/en/ who_we_are/timeline [Accessed 28 November 2012].

Interbrand (2012) *Best Global Brands 2012.* [Online]. Available from: http://www.interbrand.com/en/news-room/press-releases/2012-10-02-7543da7 .aspx [Accessed 24 November 2012].

Investopedia.com (2012) *Mass Market Retailer.* [Online]. Available from: http://www.investopedia.com/terms/m/mass-market-retailer.asp#axzz2BHSGVYnA [Accessed 28 November 2012].

Jankowicz, A. (2005) *Business Research Projects*. 4th edition. London: Thomson Learning.

Jäckel, M. (2008) *Medienwirkungen*, 4th Edition, Wiesbaden: VS Verlag.

Junghenn, S. (2012) *How To Build A Successful Social Media Strategy*.[Blog entry]. Available from: http://socialmediatoday.com/samuel-junghenn/683656/how-build-successful-social-media-strategy [Accessed 24 November 2012].

Kalra, D. (2011) Straddling Two Worlds: Luxury brand Burberry reinvented itself by combining the traditional with the digital, *Business Today*, 12 (11), pp. 62-64.

Kaplan, A. and Haenlein, M. (2010) *Users of the world, unite! The challenges and opportunities of Social Media.* Paris: ESCP Europe.

Kirklees (2012) *Research & Consultation Guidelines.* [Online]. Available from: http://www.kirklees.gov.uk/community/yoursay/Questionnaires.pdf [Accessed 25 November 2012]

Knowthis.com (2012) *Primary Research - Advantages.* [Online]. Available from: http://www.knowthis.com/principles-of-marketing-tutorials/data-collection-primary-research-methods/primary-research-advantages/ [Accessed 24 November 2012].

Laurent, F. (2012) *Social Media: the Main Runway for Fashion Industry.* [Blog entry]. Available from: http://socialmediatoday.com/laurentfrancois/439803/social-media-main-runway-fashion-industry [Accessed 24 November 2012].

Lazarsfeld, P. F. and Katz, E. (1955) *Personal Influence: The Part Played by People in the Flow of Mass Communications*, Glencoe, IL: Free Press.

Lazarsfeld, P.F. (1957) Public Opinion and the Classical Traditon, *The Public Opinion Quarterly*, 21 (1), pp. 39-53.

Lazarsfeld, P. F., Berelson, B. and Gaudet, H. (1968) *The People's Choice. How the Voter Makes up His Mind in a Presidential Campaign*, 3rd edition. New York: Columbia University Press.

Lee, M. K. O., Cheung, C. M. .K, Lim, K. H. and Sia, C. L. (2006) Understanding customer knowledge sharing in web-based discussion boards: An exploratory study, *Internet Research,* 16 (3), pp. 289-303.

Lee, T., Leung C., Zhang Z. (no date) Fashion Brand Image Marketing: Brand Image and Brand Personality, Vol. 4, No. 2. Hong Kong: RJTA.

Lenz, F. (1957) *Die Entstehung öffentlicher Meinungen, in: Gewerkschaftliche Monatshefte,* issue 9 (September), p. 520-525, [Online]. Available from http://library.fes.de/gmh/ main/pdf-files/gmh/1957/1957-09-a-520.pdf [Accessed 25 March 2012].

Levy, S.J. (1958) Symbols by which we buy, Advancing Marketing Efficiency, *American Marketing Association*, pp. 409-416.

Linkedin (2012) *Gucci.* [Online]. Available from: https://www.linkedin.com/company/gucci [Accessed 28 November 2012].

Louisvuitton (2012) *About Our Company.* [Online]. Available from: http://www.louisvuitton-hr.com/en/recruit/index.htm [Accessed 28 November 2012].

LVMH (2012) *The Group.* [Online]. Available from: http://www.lvmh.com/the-group/lvmh-group [Accessed 28 November 2012].

Managementguide (2012) *Secondary Data.* [Online]. Available from: http://www.managementstudyguide.com/secondary data.htm [Accessed 25 November 2012].

Manning-Schaffel, V. (2004) *Zara.* [Blog entry]. Available from: http://www.brandchannel.com/features webwatch.asp?ww id=190 [Accessed 28 November 2012].

Marketingcharts (2012) *Most Companies Say Social Media's Impact Tough to Measure.* [Online]. Available from: http://www.marketingcharts.com/wp/direct /most-companies-finding-social-medias-impact-tough-to-measure-23213/ [Accessed 25 November 2012].

Marketingsprofs.com (2011) *YouTube Tops Facebook, Twitter in User Satisfaction.* [Online]. Available from: http://www.marketingprofs.com/charts/2011/4549/ youtube-tops-facebook-twitter-in-user-satisfaction [Accessed 28 November2012].

Massimodutti (2012) *History of the Brand.* [Online]. Available from: http://www.massimodutti.com/webapp/wcs/stores/servlet/GeneralMSpotView?ca talogId=30210027&langId=1&storeId=34009456&footer=true&item=0&namesMSp ot=MD2_ESpot_Menu_Empresa;MD2_ESpot_Contenido_HistoriaDeLaMarca;MD2_ ESpot_Imagen_HistoriaDeLaMarca [Accessed 28 November 2012].

McCarthy, R. (2012) *The Importance of Social Media ROI.* [Online]. Available from: http://www.cmswire.com/cms/customer-experience/the-importance-of-social-media-roi-014935.php [Accessed 2 December 2012].

Mewe, R. and Heerden, G. (2009) Finding and utilizing Opinion Leaders: Social networks and the power of relationships, *S.Afr.J.Bus.Mangage.*, 40 (3), pp. 65-76.

Misner, I.R. (1999) *The World's Best Known Marketing Secret: Building Your Business with World-of-Mouth Marketing*, 2d edition. Austin: Bard Press.

Mooi, E. and Sarstedt, M. (2011) A Concise Guide to Market Research: The process, data, and methods using IBM SOSS Statistics, 1st ed., Germany: Springer.

Netmba.com (2010) *The Marketing Mix: The 4P's of Marketing.* [Online]. Available from: http://www.netmba.com/marketing/mix/ [Accessed 28 November 2012].

Nielsen (2011) *State of the Media: The Social Media Report Q3 2011.* [Online]. Available from: http://blog.nielsen.com/nielsenwire/social/ [Accessed 24 November 2012].

Noelle-Neumann, E. (1979) Public Opinion and the Classical Tradition: A Re-evaluation, *The Public Opinion Quarterly*, 43 (2), pp. 143-156.

Noelle-Neumann, E. (1980) The Public Opinion: Research Correspondent, *The Public Opinion Quarterly*, 44 (4), p. 585-597.

Noelle-Neumann, E. (1996) Öffentliche Meinung. Die Entdeckung der Schweigespirale, Frankfurt am Main: Ullstein.

Noelle-Neumann, E. (2001) Die Schweigespirale: Öffentliche Meinung – unsere soziale Haut, München: Herbig.

O'Reilly, T. (2005) *What is Web 2.0 – Design Patterns and Business Models for the Next Generation of Software*, published online 30.09.2005, http://www.oreilly.de/artikel/ web20.html. [Accessed 25 March 2012].

Ouwersloot, H. and Odekerken-Schroder, G. (2008) Who's who in brand communities – and why?, *European Journal of Marketing,* 42 (5/6), pp. 571-585.

Owyang, J. (2012a) *Build your own "IdeaStorm" with UserVoice.* [Online]. Available from: http://www.web-strategist.com/blog/2008/05/02/build-your-own-ideastorm-with-uservoice/ . [Accessed 25 March 2012].

Owyang, J. (2012b) *A Chronology of Brands that Got Punk'd by Social Media.* [Online]. Available from: http://www.web-strategist.com/blog/2008/05/02/a-chonology-of-brands-that-got-punkd-by-social-media/. [Accessed 28 April 2012].

Owyang, J. (2012c) *Matrix: Companies Should Factor 'Social Influence' Into Total Customer Value.* [Online]. Available from: http://www.web-strategist.com/blog /2010/02/03/matrix-companies-should-factor-social-influence-in-total-customer-lifetime-value/. [Accessed 25 March 2012].

Owyang, J. (2012d) *Louis Vuitton gets Brand-Jacked, Collateral Damage in Anti-Genocide Campaign.* [Online]. Available from: http://www.web-strategist.com/blog /2008/05/04/louis-vuitton-gets-brand-jacked-victimized-in-anti-genocide-campaign-tough-spot-to-be-in/. [Accessed 29 April 2012].

Oxforddictionaries.com (2012) *Definition Brand.* [Online]. Available from: http://oxforddictionaries.com/definition/english/brand?q=Brand [Accessed 28 November 2012].

Peters, L. (1998) The new interactive media: one-to-one, but who to whom?, *Marketing Intelligence & Planning,* 16 (1), pp. 22-30.

Precourt, G. (2008) Listen up: how access to digital media is transforming consumer research, *World Advertising Research Centre,* [Online]. Available from: *WARC.* http://warc.com [Accessed 14 March 2012].

Pull&Bear (2012) Company *Concept: An Ever Young Community.* [Online]. Available from:http://www.pullandbear.com/webapp/wcs/stores/servlet/category/pullandbe argb/en/pullandbear/57003?subsectionId=company_01_01 [Accessed 28 November 2012].

Reiss (2012) *About Us: The Brand.* [Online]. Available from: http://www.reiss.com/feature/brand/ [Accessed 28 November 2012].

Reuters (2012) *Gucci Group NV.* [Online]. Available from: http://in.reuters.com/ finance/stocks/companyProfile?symbol=GUCG.PK [Accessed 28 November 2012].

Responding to crisis using Social Media: Updating "Dell Hell" case study (2007) [Online]. Available from http://www.marketsentinel.com/wp-content/uploads/ Crisisresponseusing social media .pdf. [Accessed 25 March 2012].

Riegner, C. (2007) Word of Mouth on the Web: The Impact of Web 2.0 on Consumer Purchase Decisions, *Journal of Advertising Research*, December, pp.436-447

Robson, W. (1997) *Strategic management & information systems.* 2nd ed. Harlow: Pearson Education Limited.

Rogers, E.M. (2003) *Diffusion of Innovations*, 5th edition. New York: Free Press.

Saunders, M., Lewis, P. and Thornhill, A. (2009) *Research methods for business students.* 5th ed. Harlow: Pearson Education Limited.

Schermerhorn, J (2010) *Exploring Management.* 2nd ed. Hoboken: John Wiley & Sons.

Schenk, M. (1995) Soziale Netzwerke und Massenmedien: Untersuchungen zum Einfluß der persönlichen Kommunikation, Tübingen: Mohr Verlag.

Schenk, M., Dahm, H. and Sonje, D. (1996) Innovationen im Kommunikationssystem. Eine empirische Studie zur Diffusion von Datenübertragung und Mobilfunk, Münster: LIT.

Schultz, D. E. (2008) Actions, Not Promises: the future ain't going to be like the past, *Marketing Management,* March/April, pp. 10-11.

Shearman, S. (2012) *Nike poaches Burberry social-media chief Musa Tariq.* [Blog entry]. Available from: http://www.brandrepublic.com/news/1148178/nike-poaches-burberry-social-media-chief-musa-tariq/ [Accessed 24 November 2012].

Smith, T., Coyle J. R., Lightfoot E and Scott A. (2007) Reconsidering Models of Influence: the Relationship between Consumer Social Networks and Word-o-Mouth Effectiveness, *Journal of Advertising Research, December,* pp. 387-397

Smith, T. (2009) The social media revolution, *International Journal of Market Research,* 51 (4), pp. 559-561.

Smith, S. (2010) Fans have gone ape over Nestlé's Facebook profile, *Marketing Week,* 33 (14), pp. 12-12.

Socialbakers (2012a) *What brand categories lead marketing on Facebook.* [Online]. Available from: http://www.socialbakers.com/blog/266-what-brand-categories-lead-marketing-on-facebook/. [Accessed 29 April 2012].

Socialbakers (2012b) *United Kingdom Facebook Statistics.* [Online]. Available from: http://www.socialbakers.com/facebook-statistics/united-kingdom [Accessed 29 April 2012].

Socialbakers (2012c) *New in Socialbakers Analytics: Engagement Metrics That Go Deeper Into Your Page's Engagement.* [Online]. Available from: http://www.socialbakers.com/blog/484-new-in-socialbakers-analytics-engagement-metrics-that-go-deeper-into-your-page-s-engagement [Accessed 29 November 2012].

Stanoevska-Slabeva, K. (2008) Web 2.0 – Grundlagen, Auswirkungen und zukünftige Trends, in: Meckel, M. and Stanoevska-Slabeva, K. (eds.): *Web 2.0 – Die nächste Generation Internet.* Baden-Baden: Nomos, pp. 14-38.

Stelzner, M. (2012) *Social Media Marketing Industry Report 2012: How Marketers Are Using Social Media to Grow Their Business.* [Blog entry]. Available from: http://www.socialmediaexaminer.com/SocialMediaMarketingIndustryReport2012.pdf [Accessed 10 October 2012].

Summers, J. O. (1970) The Identity of Women's Clothing Fashion Opinion Leaders, *Journal of Marketing Research*, 7 (3), pp. 178-185.

Sweeney, J. C., Soutar, G. N. and Mazzarol, T. (2008) Factors influencing word of mouth effectiveness, *European Journal of Marketing*, 42 (3/4), pp. 344-364.

Tenayagroup.com (2012) How *to define Brand Engagement.* [Online]. Available from: http://www.persuasivebrands.com/Topics_Brand_Definition.aspx [Accessed 28 November 2012].

Thenonprofittimes.com (2012) *Advantages and disadvantages to 1-on-1 interview.* [Online]. Available from: http://www.thenonprofittimes.com/article/detail/advantages-and-disadvantages-to-1-on-1-interviews-4535 [Accessed 28 November 2012].

Topshop (2012) *History.* [Online]. Available from: http://www.topshop.com/webapp/wcs/stores/servlet/CatalogNavigationSearchResultCmd?catalogId=33057&

storeId=12556&langId=1&viewAllFlag=false&categoryId=273012&interstitial=true&i
ntcmpid=W_FOOTER_WK45_HP_UK_ABOUT_US [Accessed 28 November 2012].

Trusov, M., Bucklin, R. E. and Pauwels, K. (2009) Effects of World-Of-Mouth Versus Traditional Marketing: Findings from an Internet Social Networking Site, *Journal of Marketing*, 73 (5), pp. 90-102.

Turban, E. et al. (2006) *Information technology for management: transforming organizations in the digital economy*. 5th ed. Hoboken: John Wiley & Sons, Inc.

Turban, E., Sharda, R. and Delen, D. (2011) *Decision support and business intelligence systems*. 9th ed. New Jersey: Pearson Education, Inc.

Twitter (2012a) *About us*. [Online]. Available from: *https://twitter.com/about*. [Accessed 03 April 2012].

Twitter (2012b) *What is Twitter?*. [Online]. Available from: https://business.twitter .com/de/basics/what-is-twitter/ [Accessed 28 November 2012].

Uitz, I. (2012) Social Media - Is It Worth the Trouble?, *Journal of Internet Social Networking & Virtual Communities*. Graz: IBIMA Publishing.

Watts, D.J. and Dodds,P.S. (2007) Influentials, Networks, and Public Opinion Formation, *Journal of Consumer Research*, 34 (4), pp. 441-458.

Weber, H. (2012) *How the Fashion Industry Is Embracing Social Media*. [Online]. Available from: http://thenextweb.com [Accessed 24 November 2012].

Wordpress (2012). [Online]. Available from: *http://wordpress.com/* [Accessed 28 November 2012].

Youtube (2012) *Press Statistics*. [Online]. Available from: http://www.youtube.com /t/pressstatistics [Accessed 28 November 2012].

Index of Appendices

Appendix A:

Results Online Observations

Figure A1 Social Media Fans Total

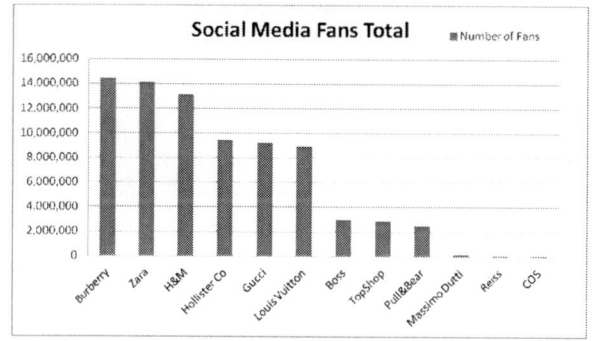

Figure A2 Social Media Engagement Total

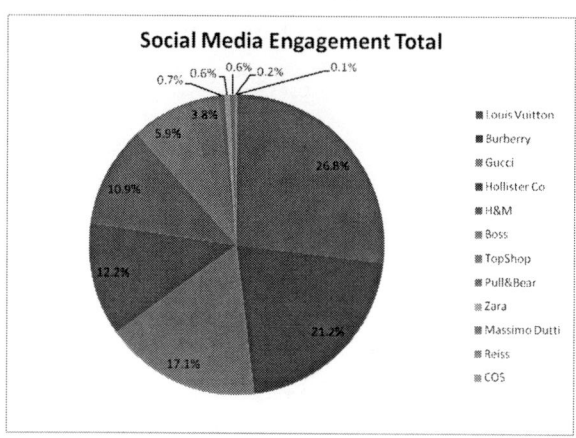

Figure A3 Social Media Posts Total

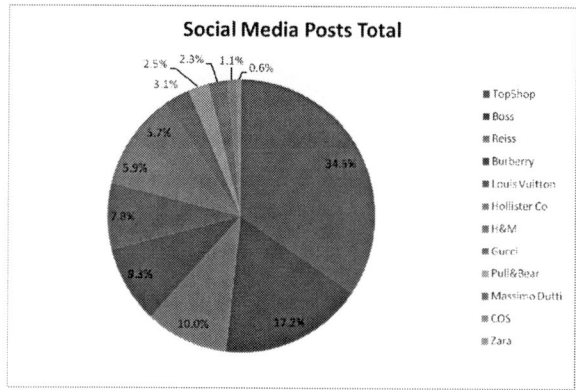

Figure A4 Facebook Fans

Facebook Fans

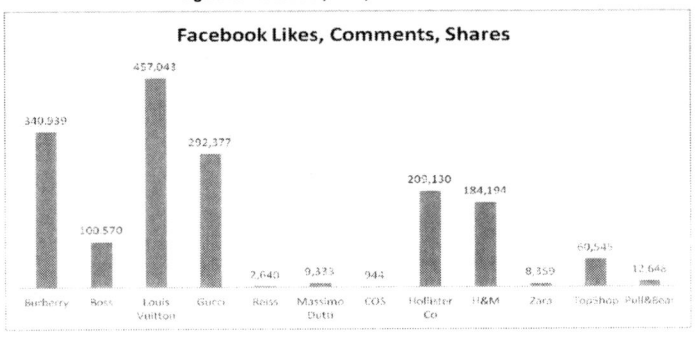

Burberry: 13,205,100
Boss: 2,839,473
Louis Vuitton: 8,678,805
Gucci: 8,784,526
Reiss: 65,123
Massimo Dutti: 171,673
COS: 28,008
Hollister Co: 9,107,314
H&M: 11,718,174
Zara: 14,105,658
TopShop: 2,453,338
Pull&Bear: 2,453,001

Figure A5 Facebook, Likes, Comments & Shares

Facebook Likes, Comments, Shares

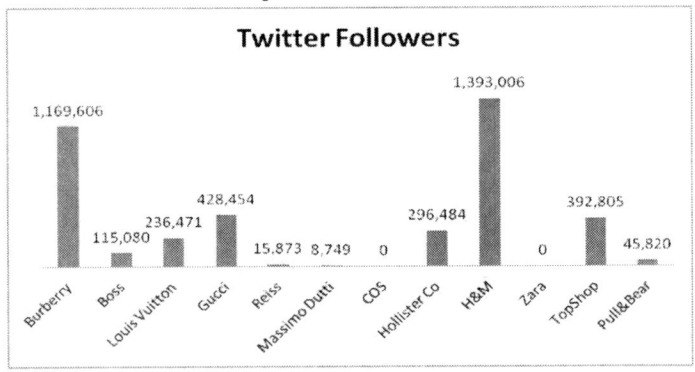

Burberry: 349,939
Boss: 100,570
Louis Vuitton: 457,048
Gucci: 292,377
Reiss: 2,640
Massimo Dutti: 9,323
COS: 944
Hollister Co: 209,130
H&M: 184,194
Zara: 8,359
TopShop: 69,545
Pull&Bear: 12,648

Figure A6 Twitter Followers

Twitter Followers

Burberry: 1,169,606
Boss: 115,080
Louis Vuitton: 236,471
Gucci: 428,454
Reiss: 15,873
Massimo Dutti: 8,749
COS: 0
Hollister Co: 296,484
H&M: 1,393,006
Zara: 0
TopShop: 392,805
Pull&Bear: 45,820

Figure A7   Twitter Retweets & Replies

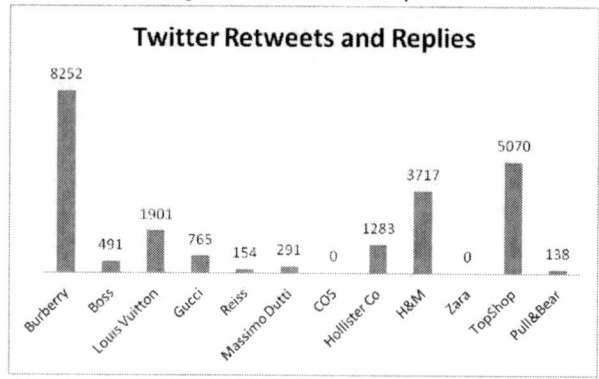

Figure A7   Twitter Retweets & Replies

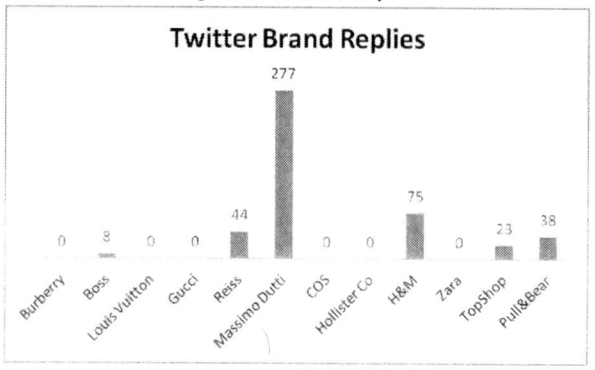

Figure A8   Twitter Brand Replies

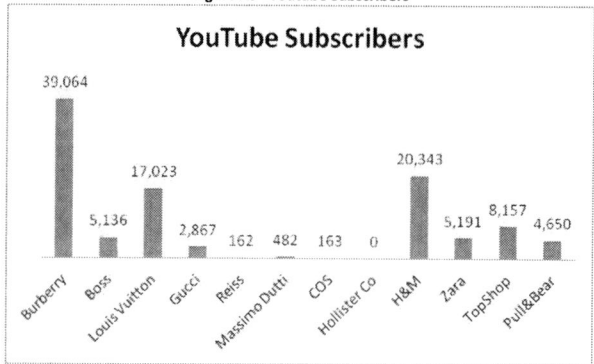

Figure A9   Youtube Subscribers

Figure A10 Youtube Likes, Dis-Likes & Comments

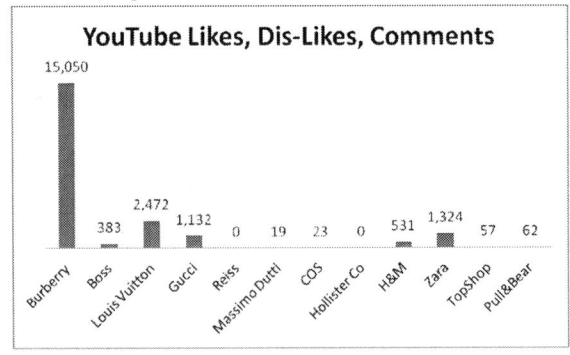

Figure A11 Youtube VideoViews

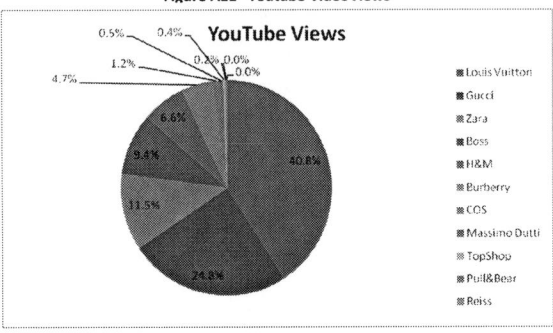

Table A1 Social Media Fans

Social Media Presence

	Facebook Fans			Twitter Followers			Youtube Subscribers			Total
	Month 1	Month 2		Month 1	Month 2		Month 1	Month 2		
Burberry	13,000,574	13,205,100	204,526	1,101,246	1,169,606	68,360	37,568	39,064	1,496	14,413,770
Boss	2,454,713	2,839,473	384,760	94,319	115,080	20,761	4,938	5,136	198	2,959,689
Louis Vuitton	8,027,676	8,678,805	651,129	199,194	236,471	37,277	14,500	17,023	2,523	8,932,299
Gucci	8,573,593	8,784,526	210,933	406,784	428,454	21,670	2,700	2,867	167	9,215,847
Reiss	62,775	65,123	2,348	15,280	15,873	593	155	162	7	81,158
Massimo Dutti	163,071	171,673	8,602	8,164	8,749	585	448	482	34	180,904
COS	26,011	28,008	1,997	-	-	-	148	163	15	28,171
Hollister Co	8,761,711	9,107,314	345,603	268,346	296,484	28,138	-	-	-	9,403,798
H&M	11,411,032	11,718,174	307,142	1,286,033	1,393,006	106,973	18,123	20,343	2,220	13,131,523
Zara	13,786,949	14,103,638	316,689	-	-	-	4,689	5,191	502	14,108,829
TopShop	2,401,862	2,453,336	51,474	369,825	392,805	22,980	6,852	8,157	1,305	2,854,298
Pull&Bear	2,391,435	2,453,001	61,566	43,877	45,820	1,943	4,485	4,650	165	2,503,471

Table A2.1 Brand Fans Total

Fans Total (Sorted)

12	Burberry	14,413,770	18.5
11	Zara	14,108,829	18.1
10	H&M	13,131,523	16.9
9	Hollister Co	9,403,798	12.1
8	Gucci	9,215,847	11.8
7	Louis Vuitton	8,932,299	11.5
6	Boss	2,959,689	3.8
5	TopShop	2,854,298	3.7
4	Pull&Bear	2,503,471	3.2
3	Massimo Dutti	180,904	0.2
2	Reiss	81,158	0.1
1	COS	28,171	0.0
		77,813,757	1.0

Table A3.1 Facebook Fans

Facebook Growth (Sorted)

Zara	13,786,949	316,689	14,103,638
Burberry	13,000,574	204,526	13,205,100
H&M	11,411,032	307,142	11,718,174
Hollister Co	8,761,711	345,603	9,107,314
Gucci	8,573,593	210,933	8,784,526
Louis Vuitton	8,027,676	651,129	8,678,805
Boss	2,454,713	384,760	2,839,473
TopShop	2,401,862	51,474	2,453,336
Pull&Bear	2,391,435	61,566	2,453,001
Massimo Dutti	163,071	8,602	171,673
Reiss	62,775	2,348	65,123
COS	26,011	1,997	28,008

Table A2.2 Brand Posts Total

Posts Total (Sorted)

12	TopShop	428	34.5
11	Boss	214	17.2
10	Reiss	124	10.0
9	Burberry	116	9.3
8	Louis Vuitton	97	7.8
7	Hollister Co	73	5.9
6	H&M	71	5.7
5	Gucci	38	3.1
4	Pull&Bear	31	2.5
3	Massimo Dutti	28	2.3
2	COS	14	1.1
1	Zara	8	0.6
		1242	100.0

Table A3.2 Twitter Followers

Twitter Growth (Sorted)

H&M	1,286,033	106973	1,393,006
Burberry	1,101,246	68360	1,169,606
Gucci	406,784	21670	428,454
TopShop	369,825	22980	392,805
Hollister Co	268,346	28138	296,484
Louis Vuitton	199,194	37277	236,471
Boss	94,319	20761	115,080
Pull&Bear	43,877	1943	45,820
Reiss	15,280	593	15,873
Massimo Dutti	8,164	585	8,749
COS	-	-	-
Zara	-	-	-

Table A2.3 Engagement Total

Engagement Total (Sorted)

12	Louis Vuitton	461,416	26.8
11	Burberry	364,241	21.2
10	Gucci	294,274	17.1
9	Hollister Co	210,413	12.2
8	H&M	188,442	10.9
7	Boss	101,444	5.9
6	TopShop	65,672	3.8
5	Pull&Bear	12,848	0.7
4	Zara	9,683	0.6
3	Massimo Dutti	9,643	0.6
2	Reiss	2,794	0.2
1	COS	967	0.1
		1,721,837	100

Table A3.3 Youtube Subscriber

Youtube Growth (Sorted)

Burberry	37,568	1496	39,064
H&M	18,123	2220	20,343
Louis Vuitton	14,500	2523	17,023
TopShop	6,852	1305	8,157
Zara	4,689	502	5,191
Boss	4,938	198	5,136
Pull&Bear	4,485	165	4,650
Gucci	2,700	167	2,867
Massimo Dutti	448	34	482
COS	148	15	163
Reiss	155	7	162
Hollister Co	-	-	-

Table A4.1 Average Engagement Rate

Average Engagement Rate

	Facebook	Twitter	Youtube	
Burberry	0.0890	0.0088	5.5038	3.9506
Boss	0.0984	0.0028	0.2868	0.0134
Louis Vuitton	0.1950	0.0187	0.5378	0.0192
Gucci	0.1447	0.0128	39.4838	0.3911
Reiss	0.1351	0.0103	0.0000	0.0000
Massimo Dutti	0.2364	1.1087	1.9710	0.1766
COS	0.3064	-	4.7035	0.0544
Hollister Co	0.0547	0.0140	-	-
H&M	0.0366	0.0121	0.4350	0.1156
Zara	0.0148	-	6.3764	0.2474
TopShop	0.0263	0.0039	0.3494	0.6205
Pull&Bear	0.0303	0.0232	1.3333	2.7470

Table A4.2 Average Response Rate

Average Response Rate

	Facebook	Twitter	Youtube	
Burberry	2.5819	0.7055	38.5265	27.6543
Boss	3.5419	0.4267	7.4572	0.3487
Louis Vuitton	5.2662	0.8039	14.5215	0.5186
Gucci	3.3283	0.1785	39.4838	0.3911
Reiss	4.0539	0.9702	0.0000	0.0000
Massimo Dutti	5.4365	3.3261	3.9419	0.3532
COS	3.3705	-	14.1104	0.1633
Hollister Co	2.2963	0.4327	-	-
H&M	1.5719	0.2668	2.6102	0.6936
Zara	0.0593	-	25.5057	0.9898
TopShop	2.4679	1.2907	0.6988	1.2410
Pull&Bear	0.5156	0.3012	1.3333	2.7470

Table A5.1 Facebook Posts

Number of posts — daily breakdown (days 1–31, Sunday–Tuesday bands) with Total column.

Brand	Total
Burberry	29
Boss	16
Louis Vuitton	27
Gucci	23
Reiss	30
Massimo Dutti	23
COS	11
Hollister Co	42
H&M	43
Zara	4
TopShop	94
Pull&Bear	17

Table A5.2   Facebook Photos & Videos

Number of impressions	1 Sunday	2 Monday	3 Tuesday	4 Wednesday	5 Thursday	6 Friday	7 Saturday	8 Sunday	9 Monday	10 Tuesday
Burberry	0	0	1	3	1	1	0	0	1	2
Boss	1	1	0	1	1	3	1	1	0	1
Louis Vuitton	0	1	1	1	1	2	1	1	2	1
Gucci	0	2	1	1	1	1	0	0	1	1
Reiss	0	0	2	1	1	1	1	1	1	1
Massimo Dutti	0	1	1	1	1	1	1	0	0	2
COS	0	1	0	0	0	0	1	0	0	0
Hollister Co	1	0	0	1	1	2	1	0	1	0
H&M	0	2	2	3	3	1	1	1	1	3
Zara	0	0	0	0	1	0	0	0	0	0
TopShop	0	7	3	5	2	4	0	0	2	6
Pull&Bear	0	1	1	1	0	2	0	1	0	0

	11 Wednesday	12 Thursday	13 Friday	14 Saturday	15 Sunday	16 Monday	17 Tuesday	18 Wednesday	19 Thursday	20 Friday	21 Saturday
Burberry	1	0	0	0	1	1	1	2	0	1	0
Boss	3	1	0	1	0	2	2	2	1	2	1
Louis Vuitton	1	1	0	1	0	2	1	1	2	1	0
Gucci	1	1	0	0	0	0	1	1	1	0	0
Reiss	1	0	1	1	1	1	1	1	1	0	1
Massimo Dutti	1	0	1	0	0	1	0	1	1	1	0
COS	0	0	1	0	0	1	0	1	1	1	0
Hollister Co	2	2	1	1	1	1	1	1	2	1	2
H&M	1	2	1	0	0	2	2	2	2	1	0
Zara	0	0	1	0	0	0	1	0	0	0	0
TopShop	2	3	5	0	0	1	3	5	8	3	0
Pull&Bear	1	0	1	0	1	0	0	1	1	1	0

	22 Sunday	23 Monday	24 Tuesday	25 Wednesday	26 Thursday	27 Friday	28 Saturday	29 Sunday	30 Monday	31 Tuesday	Total
Burberry	0	1	3	2	1	2	1	1	1	3	28
Boss	0	1	1	1	2	2	0	1	2	0	36
Louis Vuitton	0	1	1	0	2	1	1	0	1	1	27
Gucci	0	1	1	3	2	1	0	0	0	1	23
Reiss	1	1	1	0	1	2	1	1	2	1	29
Massimo Dutti	0	1	0	2	1	1	0	0	1	1	22
COS	0	1	0	1	0	0	0	0	2	0	10
Hollister Co	0	1	2	1	0	0	1	2	0	1	31
H&M	0	2	2	2	1	1	0	0	7	5	43
Zara	0	1	0	0	0	0	0	0	0	0	4
TopShop	0	3	5	4	4	6	0	0	4	5	90
Pull&Bear	0	1	0	1	2	0	0	0	1	0	17

Table A5.3   Facebook Comments

Number of comments	1 Sunday	2 Monday	3 Tuesday	4 Wednesday	5 Thursday	6 Friday	7 Saturday	8 Sunday	9 Monday	10 Tuesday
Burberry	0	0	56	361	26	36	0	0	43	181
Boss	3	13	0	21	57	91	46	11	0	90
Louis Vuitton	0	432	221	45	521	50	127	256	67	422
Gucci	0	736	177	253	49	190	0	0	24	618
Reiss	1	0	5	0	5	12	1	0	6	5
Massimo Dutti	0	12	5	4	0	8	0	0	10	6
COS	0	0	0	0	0	7	0	0	0	0
Hollister Co	142	2,152	0	60	134	760	678	299	351	277
H&M	0	94	93	127	62	53	78	4	96	371
Zara	0	0	0	0	0	3	0	0	0	0
TopShop	0	124	258	587	24	21	0	0	54	239
Pull&Bear	0	24	22	15	0	41	0	0	0	0

	11 Wednesday	12 Thursday	13 Friday	14 Saturday	15 Sunday	16 Monday	17 Tuesday	18 Wednesday	19 Thursday	20 Friday	21 Saturday
Burberry	57	0	0	76	0	98	142	179	0	123	0
Boss	37	14	0	33	0	30	23	121	36	261	25
Louis Vuitton	22	94	0	145	0	2,111	179	162	155	1,549	0
Gucci	182	19	0	0	0	0	234	199	470	0	0
Reiss	2	0	0	1	0	7	3	0	0	1	1
Massimo Dutti	13	0	10	0	0	7	0	0	4	6	0
COS	0	0	0	0	0	0	0	0	11	0	0
Hollister Co	637	330	185	105	35	71	78	54	300	29	139
H&M	67	55	28	0	0	100	864	279	83	123	0
Zara	0	0	53	0	0	0	151	0	0	0	0
TopShop	98	143	20	0	0	45	66	3	54	98	0
Pull&Bear	14	0	10	0	25	0	0	5	1	68	0

	22 Sunday	23 Monday	24 Tuesday	25 Wednesday	26 Thursday	27 Friday	28 Saturday	29 Sunday	30 Monday	31 Tuesday	Total
Burberry	0	948	542	169	333	142	327	146	118	272	4,290
Boss	0	22	17	50	72	107	0	132	196	0	1,466
Louis Vuitton	294	0	0	0	319	235	523	0	196	162	8,322
Gucci	0	140	268	676	88	800	0	0	0	201	5,243
Reiss	5	3	0	0	1	31	1	391	0	2	485
Massimo Dutti	0	0	0	58	5	2	0	0	0	2	162
COS	0	1	0	4	0	0	0	0	2	0	25
Hollister Co	131	10	1,908	276	0	216	0	614	0	1,960	10,925
H&M	0	32	308	122	129	173	0	0	111	49	3,431
Zara	0	130	0	0	0	0	0	0	0	0	337
TopShop	0	32	61	24	42	31	0	0	26	48	2,099
Pull&Bear	0	7	0	4	0	72	0	0	6	0	294

Table A5.4 Facebook Likes

Number of likes	1 Sunday	2 Monday	3 Tuesday	4 Wednesday	5 Thursday	6 Friday	7 Saturday	8 Sunday	9 Monday	10 Tuesday
Burberry	0	0	3,067	12,166	2,363	91		0	342	3,089
Boss		921	0	1,987	5,325	6,512	9,191	500	5,575	1,579
Louis Vuitton	0	37,436	12,815	2,073	25,445	4,512	11,705	12,543	3,271	18,075
Gucci	0	36,896	14,622	14,382	3,947	13,578		0	6,192	25,896
Reiss	24	0	82	45	171	83	15	26	175	25
Massimo Dutti	0	678	181	132	41	413	0	0	254	128
COS	0	38	0	0	15	0	0	0	12	0
Hollister Co	4,147	800	0	1,994	4,967	32,636	1,676	751	1,032	13,066
H&M	0	2,980	5,765	10,648	8,211	5,007	7,874	35	2,510	9,191
Zara	0	0	0	0	0	0	0	0	0	0
TopShop	0	1,936	2,345	3,509	2,911	2,623	0	0	2,566	4,108
Pull&Bear	0	464	521	103	0	3,201	0	316	0	0

	11 Wednesday	12 Thursday	13 Friday	14 Saturday	15 Sunday	16 Monday	17 Tuesday	18 Wednesday	19 Thursday	20 Friday	21 Saturday
	4,335	0	0	375	0	612	31,991	25,550	0	480	0
	666	0	125	0	1,442	1,357	8,358	2,668	54,171	500
	396	5,882	0	1,898	0	67,561	14,270	11,868	11,258	28,957	0
	6,428	52	0	0	0	0	12,408	13,506	4,305	0	0
	25	0	2	83	100	108	49	66	5	24	109
	506	0	467	0	0	626	0	0	162	220	0
	0	0	0	0	0	172	0	0	246	0	0
	12,782	10,819	9,201	4,650	4,897	4,380	3,700	3,106	17,009	2,080	5,796
	5,064	1,930	860	0	0	1,957	31,048	23,984	9,088	4,190	0
	0	0	652	0	0	0	5,196	0	0	0	0
	2,030	3,356	2,122	0	0	2,356	1,658	1,203	1,150	1,800	0
	2,190	0	276	0	1,637	0	0	318	122	138	0

	22 Sunday	23 Monday	24 Tuesday	25 Wednesday	26 Thursday	27 Friday	28 Saturday	29 Sunday	30 Monday	31 Tuesday	Total
	0	948	46,547	17,072	33,689	12,742	28,125	13,471	712	12,736	292,927
	0	2,934	1,011	4,966	3,649	8,869	0	6,634	5,475	0	90,817
	36,625	0	0	0	15,721	15,521	30,483	0	16,853	13,391	427,921
	0	11,483	13,271	37,056	3,695	33,533	0	0	0	18,330	260,774
	62	62	14	0	115	166	37	229	60	37	2,085
	0	161	0	2,674	870	129	0	0	642	362	8,372
	0	84	0	191	0	0	0	0	88	0	864
	3,497	397	17,152	10,174	0	17,284	5,017	963	0	218	192,860
	0	3,290	13,588	2,305	8,911	13,137	0	0	9,380	7,299	171,615
	0	1,852	0	0	0	0	0	0	0	0	7,712
	0	1,866	412	998	645	3,687	0	0	1,398	9,011	59,250
	0	123	0	120	0	2,381	0	0	145	0	11,306

Table A6.1 Twitter Posts

Number of tweets	1 Sunday	2 Monday	3 Tuesday	4 Wednesday	5 Thursday	6 Friday	7 Saturday	8 Sunday	9 Monday	10 Tuesday
Burberry	0	2	2	2	3	0	6	1	0	3
Boss	0	2	3	3	19	50	6	1	2	4
Louis Vuitton	0	0	1	1	1	1	3	1	2	1
Gucci	0	1	1	0	0	0	0	0	0	1
Reiss	0	1	1	1	0	2	1	0	2	1
Massimo Dutti	0	0	0	0	0	0	0	0	1	1
COS	0	0	0	0	0	0	0	0	0	0
Hollister Co	0	0	1	1	1	2	0	0	0	0
H&M	0	0	1	1	1	1	1	0	1	1
Zara	0	0	0	0	0	0	0	0	0	0
TopShop	0	1	10	17	18	11	8	0	10	11
Pull&Bear	0	0	1	1	1	2	0	1	0	0

	11 Wednesday	12 Thursday	13 Friday	14 Saturday	15 Sunday	16 Monday	17 Tuesday	18 Wednesday	19 Thursday	20 Friday	21 Saturday
	4	2	6	6	0	2	1	3	4	0	0
	6	3	3	7	10	5	3	3	6	5	0
	1	3	2	0	0	2	2	3	6	0	0
	1	0	1	0	0	0	1	1	1	1	0
	1	3	1	0	0	2	3	3	4	0	0
	0	0	0	0	0	0	0	0	0	1	0
	0	0	0	0	0	0	0	0	0	0	0
	1	3	0	0	1	0	1	1	2	1	1
	1	1	1	0	0	2	1	1	1	1	0
	1	25	16	0	0	15	11	10	14	14	0
	0	0	0	0	1	0	0	1	1	0	0

	22 Sunday	23 Monday	24 Tuesday	25 Wednesday	26 Thursday	27 Friday	28 Saturday	29 Sunday	30 Monday	31 Tuesday	Total
	1	2	5	5	6	6	2	0	2	3	80
	0	4	8	7	6	7	2	0	3	0	162
	1	1	0	2	1	2	1	0	3	0	43
	0	1	1	1	1	1	0	0	1	0	14
	0	1	1	4	5	6	1	3	2	1	91
	0	0	0	0	0	0	0	0	0	0	3
											0
	0	1	1	0	1	2	1	0	1	0	31
	0	1	1	1	1	1	0	1	1	2	27
											0
	2	10	6	9	9	17	0	6	9	15	332
	0	1	0	0	0	0	0	2	0	0	13

Table A6.2 Twitter Retweets

Number of retweets	1 Sunday	2 Monday	3 Tuesday	4 Wednesday	5 Thursday	6 Friday	7 Saturday	8 Sunday	9 Monday	10 Tuesday
Burberry	0	157	56	264	319	119	105	0	171	150
Boss	0	20	12	58	114	20	0	0	10	20
Louis Vuitton	0	14	98	46	90	0	41	117	67	
Gucci	0	34	39	0	0	0	0	0	0	70
Reiss	0	1	2	5	5	2	7	1	2	1
Massimo Dutti	0	0	0	0	0	0	0	0	4	0
COS										
Hollister Co	0	0	14	27	127	26	24	0	0	30
H&M	0	3	18	41	77	66	0	0	18	46
Zara										
Topshop	0	386	246	136	342	114	0	0	312	176
Pull&Bear	0	0	36	2	3	4	0	7	0	0

	11 Wednesday	12 Thursday	13 Friday	14 Saturday	15 Sunday	16 Monday	17 Tuesday	18 Wednesday	19 Thursday	20 Friday	21 Saturday
	353	197	218	0	130	0	180	368	431	272	0
	23	13	15	0	0	16	11	13	26	14	0
	83	74	46	50	31	127	187	116	123	0	0
	78	0	0	0	0	0	0	0	88	28	0
	8	8	10	1	0	3	4	4	7	8	8
	0	0	0	0	0	0	0	0	0	3	0
	27	166	0	11	20	0	16	0	64	23	46
	79	21	75	0	0	72	2,215	175	64	84	0
	199	178	265	51	41	133	190	95	235	270	130
	5	0	0	0	7	0	0	5	0	4	0

	22 Sunday	23 Monday	24 Tuesday	25 Wednesday	26 Thursday	27 Friday	28 Saturday	29 Sunday	30 Monday	31 Tuesday	Total
	0	568	504	557	539	407	162	536	361	492	8196
	0	28	11	2	8	4	0	0	17	3	462
	0	0	97	118	44	131	0	0	119	89	1850
	0	67	67	86	39	90	0	0	0	53	759
	0	0	2	2	0	1	3	2	8	3	102
	0	0	0	0	7	0	0	0	0	0	14
											0
	28	62	107	0	102	0	0	0	27	26	1250
	0	54	94	62	73	62	0	0	90	230	3694
											0
	71	196	123	212	261	256	86	28	187	233	4980
	0	2	0	0	0	0	0	0	0	0	86

Table A6.3 Twitter User Replies

Number of user replies/posts	1 Sunday	2 Monday	3 Tuesday	4 Wednesday	5 Thursday	6 Friday	7 Saturday	8 Sunday	9 Monday	10 Tuesday
Burberry	0	5	1	5	5	1	0	0	2	0
Boss	0	1	2	2	3	0	0	0	2	0
Louis Vuitton	0	0	6	6	2	3	0	0	4	1
Gucci	0	0	0	6	0	0	0	0	0	1
Reiss	0	3	0	4	1	0	0	0	0	4
Massimo Dutti	0	41	18	11	6	6	0	0	44	12
COS										
Hollister Co	0	1	2	0	2	0	3	0	0	1
H&M	0	70	5	7	1	3	2	0	1	1
Zara	0	4	14	7	0	0	0	0	1	3
Topshop	0	0	0	1	1	0	0	0	2	5
Pull&Bear										

	11 Wednesday	12 Thursday	13 Friday	14 Saturday	15 Sunday	16 Monday	17 Tuesday	18 Wednesday	19 Thursday	20 Friday	21 Saturday
	3	1	3	1	0	2	0	4	3	0	0
	0	0	3	0	0	5	1	0	1	2	3
	1	3	0	0	0	4	2	1	1	0	0
	0	4	6	0	0	5	4	5	0	0	0
	4	2	5	0	0	26	1	0	1	20	0
	2	1	0	0	1	0	0	0	2	0	3
	0	9	3	4	2	2	3	0	1	1	2
	4	7	5	7	0	5	6	4	2	1	1
	6	2	1	0	0	1	2	8	0	0	1

	22 Sunday	23 Monday	24 Tuesday	25 Wednesday	26 Thursday	27 Friday	28 Saturday	29 Sunday	30 Monday	31 Tuesday	Total
	0	3	0	2	0	3	0	0	0	3	58
	0	5	1	0	0	2	0	0	0	0	29
	0	0	1	3	1	2	0	0	2	0	51
											8
	1	1	0	2	0	2	1	0	0	3	52
	0	30	10	3	0	5	0	0	22	3	277
											0
	0	0	0	2	0	0	0	0	0	0	24
	0	0	4	1	2	2	0	0	3	1	123
											0
	0	0	2	1	3	2	0	0	4	0	90
	0	3	0	0	2	0	0	0	0	0	52

Table A6.4 Twitter Brand Replies

Number of company replies	1 Sunday	2 Monday	3 Tuesday	4 Wednesday	5 Thursday	6 Friday	7 Saturday	8 Sunday	9 Monday	10 Tuesday
Burberry	0	0	0	0	0	0	0	0	0	0
Boss	0	4	0	2	1	0		0	0	0
Louis Vuitton	0	0	0	0	0	0	0	0	0	0
Gucci	0	0	0	0	0	0	0	0	0	0
Reiss	0	3	0	4	1	0		0	0	4
Massimo Dutti	0	41	18	11	9	8		0	44	12
COS	0	0	0	0	0	0	0	0	0	0
Hollister Co										
H&M	0	70	5	0	0	0	0	0	0	0
Zara										
Topshop		1	12	7	0	0		0	0	0
Pull&Bear	0	0	2	0	0	1		0	0	0

	11 Wednesday	12 Thursday	13 Friday	14 Saturday	15 Sunday	16 Monday	17 Tuesday	18 Wednesday	19 Thursday	20 Friday	21 Saturday
	0	0	0	0	0	0	0	0	0	0	0
	0	0	0	0	0	0	0	0	0	0	0
	0	0	0	0	0	0	0	0	0	0	0
	0	0	0	0	0	0	0	0	0	2	0
	0	3	5	1	0	4	2	0	0	0	0
	4	2	9	0	0	26	1	0	1	20	0
	0	0	0	0	0	0	0	0	0	0	0
	0	0	0	0	0	0	0	0	0	0	0
	0	0	0	0	0	0	0	0	0	0	0
	4	2	0	0	1	0	1	8	0	0	0

	22 Sunday	23 Monday	24 Tuesday	25 Wednesday	26 Thursday	27 Friday	28 Saturday	29 Sunday	30 Monday	31 Tuesday	Total
	0	0	0	0	0	0	0	0	0	0	0
	0	0	0	0	0	0	0	0	0	0	8
	0	0	0	0	0	0	0	0	0	0	0
	0	0	0	0	0	0	0	0	0	0	0
	1	1	0	2	0	2	1	0	0	5	44
	0	35	10	3	0	0	0	0	22	3	277
											0
	0	0	0	0	0	0	0	0	0	0	0
	0	0	0	0	0	0	0	0	0	0	75
											0
	0	0	0	0	0	0	0	0	0	0	23
	0	3	0	0	2	0	0	0	0	0	38

Table A7.1 Youtube Posts

Number of posts	1 Sunday	2 Monday	3 Tuesday	4 Wednesday	5 Thursday	6 Friday	7 Saturday	8 Sunday	9 Monday	10 Tuesday
Burberry	0	0	1	2	1	0	0	0	0	0
Boss	0	4	0	0	0	3	0	0	0	1
Louis Vuitton	0	1	3	0	1	1	0	0	1	1
Gucci	0	0	0	0	0	0	0	0	0	0
Reiss	0	0	0	0	0	0	0	0	0	0
Massimo Dutti	0	0	0	0	0	0	0	0	0	0
COS	0	0	0	0	0	0		0	0	0
Hollister Co										
H&M	0	0	0	0	0	0	0	0	0	0
Zara	0	0	0	1	0	0	0	0	0	0
Topshop	0	0	0	0	0	0	0	0	0	0
Pull&Bear	0	0	0	0	0	0	0	0	0	0

	11 Wednesday	12 Thursday	13 Friday	14 Saturday	15 Sunday	16 Monday	17 Tuesday	18 Wednesday	19 Thursday	20 Friday	21 Saturday
	0	0	0	0	0	0	0	0	1	0	0
	1	1	1	1	1	0	2	0	0	0	0
	0	3	1	2	0	0	1	3	1	0	0
	0	0	0	0	0	0	0	0	0	0	0
	0	0	0	0	0	0	0	0	0	0	0
	0	0	0	0	0	0	0	0	0	0	0
	0	0	0	0	0	1	0	0	0	0	0
	1	0	0	0	0	0	0	0	0	0	0
	0	0	0	0	0	0	0	0	0	0	0
	0	0	0	0	1	0	0	0	0	0	0
	0	0	0	0	0	0	0	0	0	0	0

	22 Sunday	23 Monday	24 Tuesday	25 Wednesday	26 Thursday	27 Friday	28 Saturday	29 Sunday	30 Monday	31 Tuesday	Total
	0	0	0	0	0	0	0	0	0	0	7
	0	0	1	1	10	1	0	0	1	0	26
	0	0	0	1	1	1	0	0	5	0	27
	0	0	0	0	0	0	0	0	1	0	1
	0	0	0	0	0	0	0	0	0	0	0
	0	0	0	0	0	0	0	0	0	0	2
	0	2	0	0	0	0	0	0	0	0	3
	0	0	1	2	0	0	0	0	1	1	6
	0	0	0	0	0	0	0	0	0	3	4
	0	1	0	0	0	0	0	0	0	0	2
	0	0	0	0	1	0	0	0	0	0	1

Table A7.2 Youtube Video Views

Number of views	1 Sunday	2 Monday	3 Tuesday	4 Wednesday	5 Thursday	6 Friday	7 Saturday	8 Sunday	9 Monday	10 Tuesday
Burberry	0	0	76	21,082	14,079	0			0	0
Boss	0	0	0	0	0	12,799			0	0
Louis Vuitton	0	26,062	32,756	0	39,603	4,836			6,405	107,845
Gucci	0	0	0	0	0	0			0	0
Boss	0	0	0	0	0	0				0
Massimo Dutti	0	0	5,305	0	0	0				0
COS	0	0	0	0	0	0				0
Hollister Co										
H&M	0	0	0	0	0	0				0
Zara	0	0	0	7,477	0	0				0
TopShop	0	0	0	0	0	0				0
Pull&Bear	0	0	0	0	0	0				0

	11 Wednesday	12 Thursday	13 Friday	14 Saturday	15 Sunday	16 Monday	17 Tuesday	18 Wednesday	19 Thursday	20 Friday	21 Saturday
Burberry	0	0	0		0	0	0	0	1,882	2,146	0
Boss	509	623	1,438		653	0	2,851	0	0	0	0
Louis Vuitton	0	13,460	14,335		0	0	9,317	15,926	6,186	0	0
Gucci	0	0	0		0	0	0	0	0	0	0
Boss	0	0	0		0	0	0	0	0	0	0
Massimo Dutti	0	0	0		0	0	0	0	0	0	0
COS	0	0	0		0	107	0	0	0	0	0
Hollister Co											
H&M	27,081	0	0		0	0	0	0	0	0	0
Zara	0	0	0		2,845	0	0	0	0	0	0
TopShop	0	0	0		0	0	0	0	0	0	0
Pull&Bear	0	0	0		0	0	0	0	0	0	0

	22 Sunday	23 Monday	24 Tuesday	25 Wednesday	26 Thursday	27 Friday	28 Saturday	29 Sunday	30 Monday	31 Tuesday	Total
Burberry	0	0	15,007	0	0	0			0	0	54,422
Boss	0	0	452	621	16,645	151			76,743	0	109,816
Louis Vuitton	0	0	0	2,801	38,219	15,475			132,497	0	478,675
Gucci	0	0	0	0	0	0			289,411	0	280,411
Boss	0	0	0	0	0	0			0	0	0
Massimo Dutti	0	15,781	0	0	0	0			0	0	5,380
COS	0	15,781	0	0	0	0			0	0	14,069
Hollister Co											
H&M	0	0	30,022	7,404	0	0			6,790	5,263	76,580
Zara	0	0	0	0	0	0			0	126,283	133,766
TopShop	0	293	0	0	0	0			0	0	4,593
Pull&Bear	0	0	0	2,257	0	0			0	0	2,257

Table A7.3 Youtube User Comments

Number of comments	1 Sunday	2 Monday	3 Tuesday	4 Wednesday	5 Thursday	6 Friday	7 Saturday	8 Sunday	9 Monday	10 Tuesday
Burberry	0	0	14,036	25	15	0			0	0
Boss	0	2	0	0	0	16			0	0
Louis Vuitton	0	2	13	0	2	1			0	20
Gucci	0	0	0	0	0	0			0	0
Boss	0	0	0	0	0	0			0	0
Massimo Dutti	0	3	2	0	0	0			0	0
COS	0	3	0	0	0	0			0	0
Hollister Co										
H&M	0	0	0	0	0	0			0	0
Zara	0	1	0	10	0	0			0	0
TopShop	0	3	0	0	0	0			0	0
Pull&Bear	0	0	0	0	0	9			0	0

	11 Wednesday	12 Thursday	13 Friday	14 Tuesday	15 Sunday	16 Monday	17 Tuesday	18 Wednesday	19 Thursday	20 Friday	21 Saturday
Burberry	0	0	0	0	0	0	0	0	5	0	0
Boss	0	0	7	0	0	0	0	0	0	0	0
Louis Vuitton	0	12	2	7	0	0	3	7	3	0	0
Gucci	0	0	0	0	0	0	0	0	0	0	0
Boss	0	0	0	0	0	0	0	0	0	0	0
Massimo Dutti	0	0	0	0	0	0	0	0	0	0	0
COS	0	0	0	0	0	0	0	0	0	0	0
Hollister Co											
H&M	17	0	0	0	0	0	0	0	0	0	0
Zara	0	0	0	0	0	0	0	0	0	0	0
TopShop	0	0	0	0	0	0	0	0	0	0	0
Pull&Bear	0	0	0	0	0	0	0	0	0	0	0

	22 Sunday	23 Monday	24 Tuesday	25 Wednesday	26 Thursday	27 Friday	28 Saturday	29 Sunday	30 Monday	31 Tuesday	Total
Burberry	0	0	71	0	0	0			0	0	14,151
Boss	0	0	0	0	21	1			29	0	74
Louis Vuitton	0	0	0	7	8	5			116	0	212
Gucci	0	0	0	0	0	0			176	0	176
Boss	0	0	0	0	0	0			0	0	0
Massimo Dutti	0	0	0	0	0	0			0	0	2
COS	0	1	0	0	0	0			0	0	1
Hollister Co											
H&M	0	0	15	11	0	0			11	7	61
Zara	0	0	0	0	0	0			0	12	111
TopShop	0	0	0	0	0	0			0	0	11
Pull&Bear	0	0	0	0	5	0			0	0	5

Table A7.4 Youtube Likes

Number of likes	1 Sunday	2 Monday	3 Tuesday	4 Wednesday	5 Thursday	6 Friday	7 Saturday	8 Sunday	9 Monday	10 Tuesday	11 Wednesday	12 Thursday	13 Friday	14 Saturday	15 Sunday	16 Monday	17 Tuesday	18 Wednesday	19 Thursday	20 Friday	21 Saturday	22 Sunday	23 Monday	24 Tuesday	25 Wednesday	26 Thursday	27 Friday	28 Saturday	29 Sunday	30 Monday	31 Tuesday	Total
Burberry	0	0	132	163	62	0	0	0	0	0	0	0	0	0	0	0	0	0	38	22	0	0	0	367	0	0	0	0	0	0	0	834
Boss	0	0	0	0	0	58	0	2	0	4	0	7	73	1	4	0	11	0	0	0	0	0	0	1	8	79	0	0	0	63	0	273
Louis Vuitton	0	62	169	0	58	20	0	0	15	129	0	63	20	11	0	0	30	62	36	0	0	0	0	0	54	73	28	0	0	1,083	0	2,169
Gucci	0	0	0	0	0	0	0	0	0	0	0	0	0	0	0	0	0	0	0	0	0	0	0	0	0	0	0	0	0	890	0	890
Reiss	0	0	0	0	0	0	0	0	0	0	0	0	0	0	0	0	0	0	0	0	0	0	0	0	0	0	0	0	0	0	0	0
Massimo Dutti	0	0	16	0	0	0	0	0	0	0	0	0	0	0	0	0	0	0	0	0	0	0	0	0	0	0	0	0	0	0	0	16
COS	0	0	0	0	0	0	0	0	0	0	0	0	0	0	0	3	0	0	0	0	0	0	15	0	0	0	0	0	0	0	0	21
Hollister Co	-																															-
H&M	0	0	0	0	0	0	0	0	0	0	100	0	0	0	0	0	0	0	0	0	0	0	0	155	52	0	0	0	0	70	66	444
Zara	0	0	0	71	0	0	0	0	0	0	0	0	0	0	26	0	0	0	0	0	0	0	0	0	0	0	0	0	0	0	1,100	1,171
TopShop	0	0	0	0	0	0	0	0	0	0	0	0	0	0	0	0	0	0	0	0	0	0	12	0	0	0	0	0	0	0	0	40
Pull&Bear	0	0	0	0	0	0	0	0	0	0	0	0	0	0	0	0	0	0	0	0	0	0	0	0	0	56	0	0	0	0	0	56

Table A7.5 Youtube Dis-Likes

Number of dis-likes	1 Sunday	2 Monday	3 Tuesday	4 Wednesday	5 Thursday	6 Friday	7 Saturday	8 Sunday	9 Monday	10 Tuesday	11 Wednesday	12 Thursday	13 Friday	14 Saturday	15 Sunday	16 Monday	17 Tuesday	18 Wednesday	19 Thursday	20 Friday	21 Saturday	22 Sunday	23 Monday	24 Tuesday	25 Wednesday	26 Thursday	27 Friday	28 Saturday	29 Sunday	30 Monday	31 Tuesday	Total
Burberry	0	0	1	5	4	0	0	0	0	0	0	0	0	0	0	0	0	0	1	1	0	0	0	0	0	0	0	0	0	0	0	25
Boss	0	2	0	0	0	4	0	0	0	0	0	1	0	1	1	0	0	0	0	0	0	0	0	0	0	7	0	0	0	22	0	16
Louis Vuitton	0	1	27	0	1	0	0	0	3	25	0	0	1	0	0	0	0	3	0	0	0	0	0	0	1	2	4	0	0	22	0	91
Gucci	0	0	0	0	0	0	0	0	0	0	0	0	0	0	0	0	0	0	0	0	0	0	0	0	0	0	0	0	0	66	0	66
Reiss	0	0	0	0	0	0	0	0	0	0	0	0	0	0	0	0	0	0	0	0	0	0	0	0	0	0	0	0	0	0	0	0
Massimo Dutti	0	0	1	0	0	0	0	0	0	0	0	0	0	0	0	0	0	0	0	0	0	0	0	0	0	0	0	0	0	0	0	1
COS	0	0	0	0	0	0	0	0	0	0	0	0	0	0	0	0	0	0	0	0	0	0	1	0	0	0	0	0	0	0	0	1
Hollister Co	-																															-
H&M	0	0	0	0	0	0	0	0	0	0	0	0	0	0	0	0	0	0	0	0	0	0	0	14	3	0	0	0	0	5	0	26
Zara	0	0	0	2	0	0	0	0	0	0	0	0	0	0	0	5	0	0	0	0	0	0	0	0	0	0	0	0	0	0	11	20
TopShop	0	2	0	0	0	0	0	0	0	0	0	0	0	0	0	0	0	0	0	0	0	0	0	0	0	0	0	0	0	0	0	6
Pull&Bear	0	0	0	0	0	0	0	0	0	0	0	0	0	0	0	0	0	0	0	0	0	0	0	0	0	1	0	0	0	0	0	1

Table A8 Top 3 Brands

Top 3 Facebook
Louis Vuitton
Boss
Hollister Co
Top 3 Twitter
H&M
Burberry
Louis Vuitton
Top 3 Youtube
Louis Vuitton
H&M
Burberry
Top 3 Total
Burberry
Zara
H&M

Table A9   Facebook Shares per Month

Number of shares	Monthly
Burberry	43722
Boss	8287
Louis Vuitton	20800
Gucci	17360
Reiss	70
Massimo Dutti	799
COS	55
Hollister Co	5555
H&M	7148
Zara	310
TopShop	3196
Pull&Bear	1048

Table A10.1   Facebook Average Post Rate

		Posts	
1	TopShop	94	
2	H&M	43	
3	Hollister Co	42	
4	Boss	36	
5	Reiss	30	
6	Burberry	29	
7	Louis Vuitton	27	
8	Gucci	23	
9	Massimo Dutti	23	
10	Pull&Bear	17	
11	COS	11	
12	Zara	4	
	Mean	31.5833333	Month
		1.0188172	Day

Table A10.1   Twitter Average Post Rate

1	TopShop	332	
2	Boss	152	
3	Reiss	94	
4	Burberry	80	
5	Louis Vuitton	43	
6	Hollister Co	31	
7	H&M	22	
8	Gucci	14	
9	Pull&Bear	13	
10	Massimo Dutti	3	
11	COS	0	
12	Zara	0	
	Mean	78.4	Month
		2.52903226	Day

Appendix B:

Results User Questionnaire

Question 1:

Which of the following Social Media platforms are you aware of ?

1. Which of the following Social Media platforms are you aware of:			
	answered question	**50**	
	skipped question	**0**	
	Response Total	Response Count	Response Mean
Facebook	100.0%	51	**15.4%**
YouTube	88.2%	45	13.6%
Twitter	82.4%	42	12.7%
Google+	80.4%	41	12.3%
MySpace	66.7%	34	10.2%
Instagram	54.9%	28	8.4%
Flickr	52.9%	27	8.1%
Tumblr	39.2%	20	6.0%
Fashion Blogs	31.4%	16	4.8%
Pinterest	29.4%	15	4.5%
Foursquare	19.6%	10	3.0%
Other	5.9%	3	0.9%
Total		332	100%

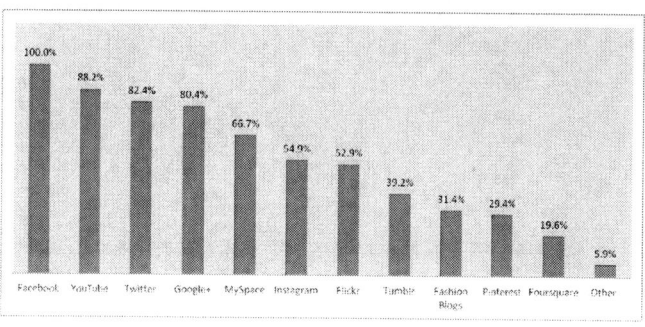

Question 2:

Which Social Media platforms are you registered with?

2. Which Social Media platforms are you registered with:			
	answered question	**50**	
	skipped question	**0**	
	Response Percent	Response Count	Response Mean
Facebook	100.0%	50	**32.9%**
YouTube	54.0%	27	17.8%
Google+	44.0%	22	14.5%
Twitter	42.0%	21	13.8%
Instagram	26.0%	13	8.6%
Pinterest	14.0%	7	4.6%
Tumblr	8.0%	4	2.6%
MySpace	6.0%	3	2.0%
Foursquare	4.0%	2	1.3%
Fashion Blogs	4.0%	2	1.3%
Flickr	2.0%	1	0.7%
Others	0.0%	0	0.0%
Total		152	100%

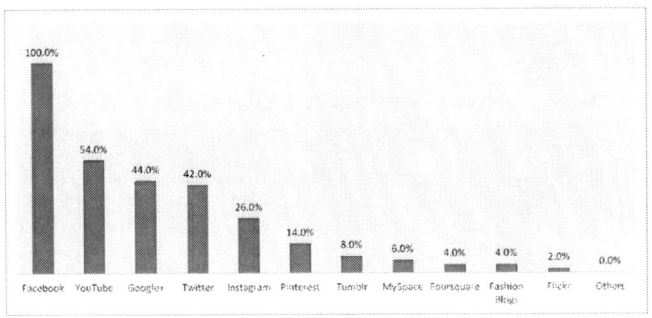

Question 3:

At what time of the day is your highest usage of your chosen Social Media platform?

3. At what time of the day is your highest usage of your chosen Social Media platforms:			
answered question		50	
skipped question		0	
	Response Percent	Response Count	Response Mean
Evening	60.0%	30	60.0%
Equally throughout the day	34.0%	13	26.0%
Afternoon	10.0%	4	8.0%
Morning	8.0%	3	6.0%
Total		50	100%

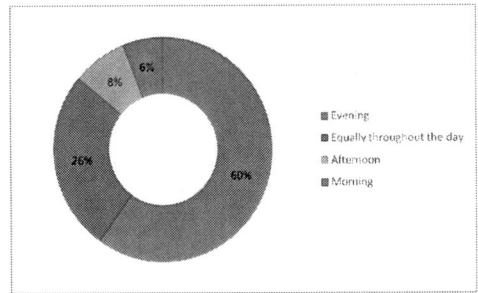

Question 4:

Please indicate your degree of activity (reading and posting) on the following Social Media platforms: (1 = not active; 5 = very active)

4. Please indicate your degree of activity (reading and posting) on the following Social Media platforms: (1 = not active ; 5 = very active)							
					answered question		50
					skipped question		0
	1	2	3	4	5	n/a	Response Count
Facebook	0.0% (0)	10.0% (5)	22.0% (11)	20.0% (10)	48.0% (24)	0.0% (0)	50
Twitter	51.4% (19)	8.1% (3)	8.1% (3)	10.8% (4)	5.4% (2)	16.2% (6)	37
Instagram	30.6% (11)	13.9% (5)	8.3% (3)	8.3% (3)	5.6% (2)	33.3% (12)	36
Pinterest	33.3% (11)	12.1% (4)	3.0% (1)	9.1% (3)	0.0% (0)	42.4% (14)	33
YouTube	21.4% (9)	21.4% (9)	26.2% (11)	19.0% (8)	7.1% (3)	4.8% (2)	42
Tumblr	38.7% (12)	3.2% (1)	3.2% (1)	6.5% (2)	3.2% (1)	45.2% (14)	31
MySpace	48.5% (16)	3.0% (1)	0.0% (0)	0.0% (0)	0.0% (0)	48.5% (16)	33
Fashion Blogs	38.7% (12)	9.7% (3)	9.7% (3)	0.0% (0)	3.2% (1)	38.7% (12)	31
Communities/Forums	50.0% (16)	6.3% (2)	3.1% (1)	3.1% (1)	0.0% (0)	37.5% (12)	32
Foursquare	38.7% (12)	6.5% (2)	0.0% (0)	0.0% (0)	0.0% (0)	54.8% (17)	31
Total							356

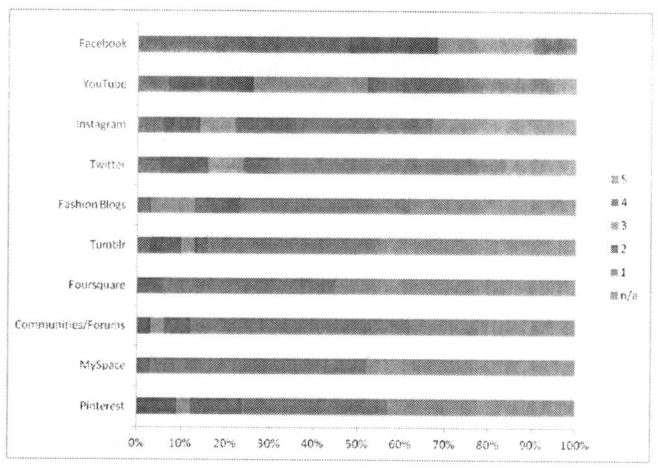

Question 5:

What activities are you participating in via Social Media?

5. What activities are you participating in via Social Media:			
	answered question	49	
	skipped question	1	
	Response Percent	Response Count	Response Mean
Liking	91.8%	45	19.9%
Commenting	89.8%	44	19.5%
Posting pictures	85.7%	42	18.6%
Sharing links	71.4%	35	15.5%
Sharing posts	55.1%	27	11.9%
Posting videos	34.7%	17	7.5%
Criticising	22.4%	11	4.9%
Other	10.2%	5	2.2%
Total		226	100%

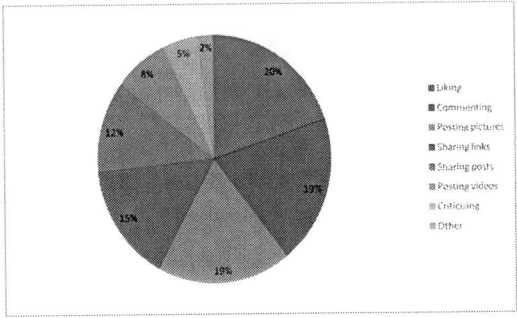

Question 6:

How much do you agree with the following sentence: By using Social Media I believe I can influence fashion companies:

6. How much do you agree with the following sentence: By using Social Media I believe I can influence fashion companies:		
	answered question	49
	skipped question	1
	Response Percent	Response Count
Strongly agree	16.3%	8
Agree	32.7%	16
Disagree	46.9%	23
Strongly disagree	4.1%	2
Total	100.0%	49

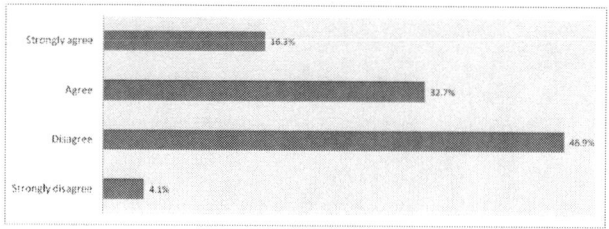

Question 7:

How much do you agree with the following sentence: By using Social Media I believe I can influence other participants regarding fashion:

7. How much do you agree with the following sentence: By using Social Media I believe I can influence other participants regarding fashion:		
answered question		49
skipped question		1
	Response Percent	Response Count
Strongly agree	20.4%	10
Agree	57.1%	28
Disagree	18.4%	9
Strongly disagree	4.1%	2
Total	100.0%	49

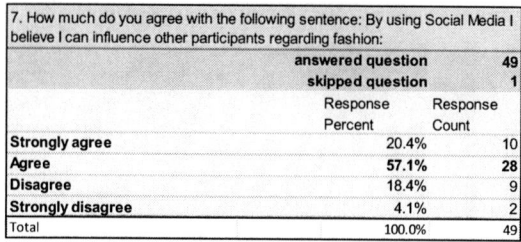

Question 8: Which of the following fashion brands do you subscribe to?

8. Which of the following fashion brands do you subscribe to:			
answered question		37	
skipped question		13	
	Response Percent	Response Count	Response Mean
H&M	62.2%	23	20.4%
Zara	59.5%	22	19.5%
TopShop	37.8%	14	12.4%
Other	35.1%	13	11.5%
Boss	21.6%	8	7.1%
Burberry	16.2%	6	5.3%
Hollister Co	16.2%	6	5.3%
Gucci	10.8%	4	3.5%
Reiss	10.8%	4	3.5%
COS	10.8%	4	3.5%
Pull&Bear	10.8%	4	3.5%
Massimo Dutti	8.1%	3	2.7%
Louis Vuitton	5.4%	2	1.8%
Total		113	100.0%

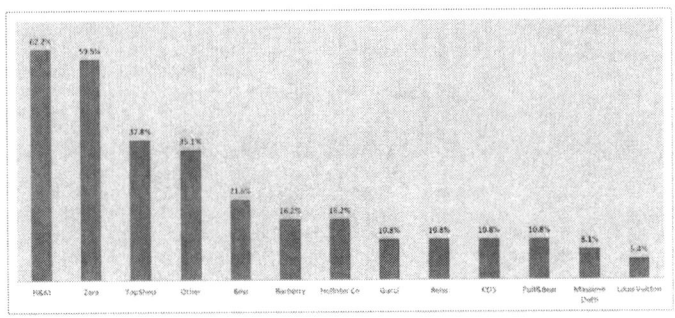

Question 9:

Why would you follow a fashion brand via Social Media?

9. Why would you follow a fashion brand via Social Media:			
	answered question	46	
	skipped question	5	
	Response Percent	Response Count	Response Mean
Other	4.3%	2	2.4%
As it is popular	6.5%	3	3.6%
I admire the brand	43.5%	20	23.8%
I want to keep up to date with the latest trends and collections	63.0%	29	34.5%
I want to recieve information about promotions, sales and store openings	65.2%	30	35.7%
Total		84	100.0%

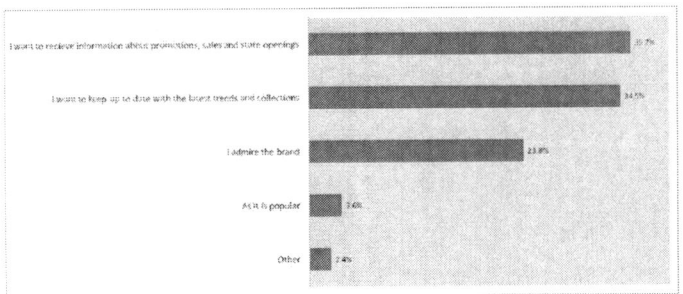

Question 10:

How do you feel Social Media adds value to a fashion company's brand?

10. How do you feel Social Media adds value to a fashion company's brand:			
answered question		45	
skipped question		6	
	Response Percent	Response Count	Response Mean
	6.7%	3	3.7%
Other			
It is a good supplement to reading fashion magazines	17.8%	8	9.9%
It is a fun way to interact with the brand	33.3%	15	18.5%
It is a good way to provide customer service	37.8%	17	21.0%
It is an easy and fast way to keep up to date with the latest trends	84.4%	38	46.9%
Total		81	100.0%

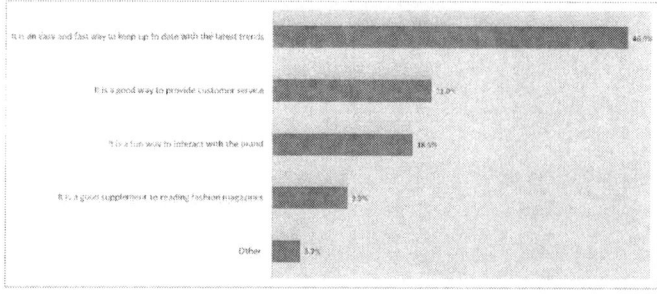

Appendix C:

Interview Questionnaire

Dear respondent

I am a postgraduate student at London South Bank University, currently writing my Masters dissertation in the UK about the importance of social media for the fashion industry for the degree International Business. I would highly appreciate, if you could spare 10-15 minutes of your time completing this survey consisting of 16 questions. The results of the study will be used for academic purposes only and your responses will be treated with absolute anonymity and confidentiality.

The main purpose of the research is to find out if it is beneficial for the fashion industry having one or different social media presences at one time, how the brands perform on social media platforms and how can their performance be measured in terms of success to improve investment in future. Therefore the main part of the research is based on an quantitative approach concerning the social media presence of 12 fashion brands. These brands consist of 4 lower priced labels, 4 medium priced labels and 4 high priced, luxury fashion labels. Over a time period of one month their social media performance at the three most popular platforms Facebook, Twitter and Youtube has been observed on a daily base.

Results have shown so far, that luxury brands have a high number of followers and getting a lot of attention in the web. But their create a minimum of daily content to engage with the users or create awareness for their brand. The low priced labels instead are using social media quite efficiently by dealing with customer concerns via twitter and included social media already in their marketing strategy by creating daily content to engage with users and the brand. It seems that the medium priced labels are still struggle with social media applications and unsure how to use it in the right way. There is often no content creation at all. The main importance and difficulty lies in how to measure the success of the brand's social media activity. At this stage there is no satisfactory measurement that can be used. Hence, this work tries to find clear statements about How to measure social media success to define the importance of social media for the Fashion Industry.

Thank you very much for your participation!
Steffen Achenbach
MSC IB London South Bank University, London

! You might answer the questions either from a specific brand perspective or from a fashion perspective !

1. Please state the previous experience you've had of using social media platforms for business purposes.

2. Which of the following social media platforms are you aware of:

- [ ] Facebook
- [ ] Twitter
- [ ] YouTube
- [ ] MySpace
- [ ] Foursquare
- [ ] Tumblr
- [ ] Flickr
- [ ] Instagram
- [ ] Pinterest
- [ ] Google+
- [ ] Fashion Blogs
- [ ] Other (please specify)

3. Tick the boxes the best represent how your company use any social media applications.

- [ ] Customer Service
- [ ] Product Promotions
- [ ] Product Information
- [ ] Company Information
- [ ] Brand Engagement
- [ ] Brand Awareness
- [ ] Other (please specify)

4. How important do you think social media is for the fashion industry and why?

5. Which of the following social media platforms is your company registered with:

- [ ] Facebook
- [ ] Twitter
- [ ] YouTube
- [ ] MySpace
- [ ] Foursquare
- [ ] Tumblr
- [ ] Flickr
- [ ] Instagram
- [ ] Pinterest
- [ ] Google+
- [ ] Fashion Blogs
- [ ] Other (please specify)

6. Why does your company engage with social media?

- [ ] Everyone else does
- [ ] Improve customer service
- [ ] Good advertising
- [ ] Improve brand image
- [ ] Don't know

7. Based on your experience, what time of the day do you think is the best to reach the most people via social media applications:

- [ ] Morning
- [ ] Afternoon
- [ ] Evening
- [ ] Equally throughout the day

8. What kind of posts do you think are the most efficient ones in terms of being reached by the largest audience:

- ☐ Picture Posts
- ☐ Campaign Posts
- ☐ Video Posts
- ☐ Statement Posts
- ☐ Link Posts
- ☐ Other (please specify)

9. How do you deal with critique and negative comments on your social media platform:

10. Do you think users can influence the public opinion about a brand via social media applications:

11. Do you think marketers can control the shared content about a brand on their own social media platform:

12. How do you measure your Return On Investment (ROI) and hence the success of your social media activities:

13. Would you be interested in a more effective method of measuring the ROI?

14. Why do you think is it important to measure a brands social media activity?

- ☐ Enhancing and understanding customer service
- ☐ Improve brand and reputation management
- ☐ Measure social media success for businesses
- ☐ Identify the most influential online users in your community
- ☐ Analyze your brand's performance compared to competitor performance
- ☐ Other (please specify)

15. Do you feel investment in your social media activities should be increased in the future?

16. In your experience are there any risks associated with using social media for your company?

-Than You-

Appendix D:

Formulas

$$Engagement\ Rate_{Facebook} = \frac{\dfrac{Likes + Comments + Shares}{\#\ of\ Wall\ Posts\ made\ by\ page}}{Total\ Fans} * 100$$

$$Engagement\ Rate_{Twitter} = \frac{\dfrac{Replies\ +\ Retweets}{\#\ of\ Tweets\ made\ by\ profile}}{Total\ Followers} * 100$$

$$Engagement\ Rate_{YouTube_1} = \frac{\dfrac{Comments\ +\ Likes\ +\ Dislikes}{\#\ of\ Posts\ made\ by\ channel}}{Total\ Subscribers} * 100$$

$$Engagement\ Rate_{YouTube_2} = \frac{\dfrac{Users\ Engaged}{\#\ of\ Posts\ made\ by\ channel}}{Users\ Reached} * 100$$

$$Response\ Rate_{Facebook} = \frac{Comments + Likes + Shares}{Total\ Fans} * 100$$

$$Response\ Rate_{Twitter} = \frac{Replies\ +\ Retweets}{Total\ Followers} * 100$$

$$Response\ Rate_{YouTube_1} = \frac{Comments\ +\ Likes\ +\ Dislikes}{Total\ Subscribers} * 100$$

$$Response\ Rate_{YouTube_2} = \frac{Comments\ +\ Likes\ +\ Dislikes}{Total\ Views} * 100$$

Supporting Documents

- ❖ Weekly Reflective Diary

- ❖ Research Proposal

CPSIA information can be obtained at www.ICGtesting.com
Printed in the USA
LVOW11s1749091114

412760LV00004B/431/P